Struggles
and
Sunshine

Confessions, Prayers, and Biblical Insights
From a Christian Mom

By
— **Trisha Nicole Ramos** —

ISBN: 978-0-9985939-1-3

First Edition

Scripture quotations taken from the New American
Standard Bible® (NASB), Copyright © 1960, 1962,
1963, 1968, 1971, 1972, 1973,
1975, 1977, 1995 by The Lockman Foundation
Used by permission. www.Lockman.org

Cover design: Chafi Charneco

Interior layout: John Manning

Lovely book, so inspiring will read it again.

—Marlene (*Trisha's mom and Grandmother of Eden Joy*)

I'm truly inspired and convicted by the example set for me in this book as a new mother.

—Amanda, *new mom*

The portion I read of "From Struggles to Sunshine" was so good...I read it twice!

—Marie, *mother of 2*

A heartfelt and very relatable read. I especially enjoyed your analogy with Eden's blanket and the covering we have in Christ! I thanked the Lord for my blanket that night.

—Carianne, *mother of 4*

A candid and biblically instructive read of one mother's diary of the first two years of her firstborn's life.

—Liz, *single Christian, hoping to be a mom one fine day*

A deeply edifying, timely admonishment for us Christian mothers.

—Michelle, *mother of 2*

Laugh, cry, and relate, are all things you'll experience when reading Trish's soul-baring journey through her first two years of motherhood. Most of all, you'll be exceedingly encouraged by her constant focus on Christ. Philippians 4:9

—Kristen, *mother of 1*

Through the Lords providence Trish and I met at a mutual friend's home. This was nearly ten years ago. Both of us at this time were without children and crazy about street evangelism, she in the US and I as a missionary in Mexico. Now the Lord has given us a few little arrows to raise up in the fear and admonition of the Lord. Seeing Trish becoming a mom has been one of the greatest answers to prayer I've ever seen! This book will take you in to the life of this dear mama, you will read about her fears, her joys, her struggles, her prayers and answers to prayer, and much more. Here you will get a glimpse of what raising a child in a Christian home looks like; you will see how a mom can turn any moment into an opportunity to point a child to Christ and His Scriptures. You will be amazed to see what a diligent mom can do with a two year old! Eden shows us that there's much more to a two year old than the terrible twos! They are much smarter than given credit for, they are cunning to do mischief but can use that same brilliant mind to learn good and do good, and instead of being a burden they can become one of your greatest joys.

—Lina Urban, *mother of 2 and missionary to Mexico*

A Word of Thanks...

My utmost thanks to the Lord who helped bring this book together and who provided the dear people that got behind it.

Thank you to my mom who read almost every word before it was published. I am thankful that she has been with me, through every high and low. This work would not be the same if you were not here, Mom. Maybe God could take us "up" at the same time as He did Enoch.

Thank you to Eden Joy. This book only exists because you exist. I thank God for 12/14/16 (the day of your birth). Your life has already proved to bless many lives, including mine, beyond measure. I love you.

And, finally, thank you to the dear ladies at Heritage Grace Community Church in Frisco, TX. Many of you have already read the preview copy, and your words of encouragement kept me writing. Thank you to Marie who told me, after I sent her a portion of the book, that she read it "twice" because she enjoyed it so much. That especially kept me writing. I hope that Marie's testimony will be the same for numerous others, for God's glory, and the edification of souls; that many will grow as godly mothers and ultimately as Christians. Onward Christian mothers!

Foreword

Godly motherhood requires a lot of focus. Just like a garden needs much tending in order for it to flourish, our children need our focused love, care, and attention. Watching my longtime friend, Trisha, experience the joys and challenges of motherhood with this kind of deep spiritual focus has been an incredible blessing to me. I am often convicted and encouraged by the amazing ways that she pours into her daughter. I am not surprised at the way Trisha puts her whole heart into being a mother, as she has always put her whole heart into everything she does for the Lord. And the same is true for this beautiful book that she has written. Her transparency, her words of encouragement, and her desire to be pleasing to the Lord will be an inspiration and blessing to every mother.

Rachel Zwayne, *mother of 5*
Daughter of Ray Comfort

Preface

*I have remembered Your ordinances from of old, O Lord,
and comfort myself."*

Psalm 119:52

You are about to embark on a look into one mom's life. The ups and downs and everything in-between. I have not left out real heart issues in this book in hopes that those of you reading this will find comfort, even as I have in the Scriptures. I like to think of this book as a diary or a journal of some of my most wonderful memories raising my daughter Eden during her first two years of life. You will also find me confessing my cares and worries and deep rooted heart issues as I work through them (things that I didn't even know where there).

This book kept me going numerous nights when my heart would ache over the thought of Eden growing up and no longer being in our house (She is only 2! I know you are thinking that. But this has been one of my big battles, I guess I just never want her to move out, and I'm sure many of you "get it"). Not all of you will battle that particular issue but maybe your big battle is your health. As is mine. You will read about my health issues and how it has affected my life as a mom on several of my day to day entries and perhaps you will learn something new or be encouraged that you are not alone as you battle with your personal health. I must admit it was easy to write this book as it helped me take my eyes off my often dizziness and fatigue and constant ringing in my ears. Just writing it night after night, with Eden on my lap in the quiet of the night when everyone was a sleep in the house, was like healing balm to my own soul. It helped to write out my cares and counsel myself in the Word (Jude 1:20, Psalm 119:52, 55). This book is as if you are peering into my own personal counseling session (not on every entry but on many of them). Who knows maybe you will feel good about yourself as you read about all my woes and you will think, "wow she has a lot of problems and my lot is not so bad after all!"

I know many of you reading this are from very solid biblical churches (as am I) and I'm confident that if you are reading this you are not too keen on "self help" books and things of this sort which tend to be very watered down and unbiblical, but we must admit our "selves" at times need a lot of help. It is my prayer that you will be empowered and uplifted in your soul as you read through this book and that you find some nuggets to chew on, some light hearted things to laugh at and biblical truths to sustain your "selves" in the road you are on. Thank you for your precious time.

> *"For of Him, and through Him, and to Him, are all things.*
> *To Him be the glory forever. Amen."*
>
> Romans 11:36

April 10, 2019
Trisha Nicole Ramos

☾ CHANGED ☽

Delight yourself in the LORD; And He will give you the desires of your heart.

Psalm 37:4

---

*S*EPTEMBER 30, 2016

I have about two more months to go for the baby to be here.

Not many of you may know this, but for almost my whole marriage I had no desire to have my own children. In fact, all growing up I wanted to live on a farm with tons of dogs and cute furry animals. I had hundreds of stuffed animals, mainly dogs with only two cabbage patch dolls and a couple of Barbies.

When God saved me, my desire to have children did not change. Instead, I only wanted to evangelize the world and pretty much die on the streets talking to people about the Lord.

Then God brought my husband Emilio into my life (in fact we met while evangelizing on the streets). I told him all I wanted to do was church ministry and preach the gospel. He didn't mind that one bit, and we got married.

So, when people would ask about my testimony, I would somewhat jokingly say, "God opened my heart, not my womb."

Then, through a series of events (major health events), God changed my heart.

The Lord is so patient and wise in how He deals with His children. His timing is always perfect, even with having a first baby at age 39.

After my heart change, I prayed to God that I could have a baby before 39 and He is answering that very specific prayer. He loves us to be specific when we pray. 1 Thessalonians 5:17 says that, "we should always pray and not lose heart." That must mean that He wants us to pray about the things that are in front of us, or on our minds and on our heart.

I have a twofold prayer for childbirth and beyond:

1. For an effortless, pain-free, heavenly, out of this world, natural birth!

2. That our child's first words will be "Christ is Lord."

Wouldn't that be amazing?

Thank you to the countless people (especially my mom and family) that prayed that we would have a child. God heard.

Let's cast our cares on Him today. Is there something that seems too difficult for God to answer? Submit it to Him. Remember He is the maker of Heaven and Earth. Your request is nothing for Him (Phil 4:6-7).

Delight yourself in the LORD; And He will give you the desires of your heart.

Psalm 37:4

❧ ANTICIPATION ❧

The steadfast of mind You will keep in perfect peace, Because he trusts in You.

Isaiah 26:3

*D*ECEMBER 6, 2016

I am due to have a baby this week. So they say.

I've felt so great, better than I have in three years, that sometimes it seems surreal, like the baby can't be coming this soon. I have been comforted beyond measure by the many kind messages, texts, comments and emails that I've received. I am confident that God is going to work effectually through everyone's prayers.

On our walk tonight, Emilio and I went to a middle school for a stroll around the track. We always let our dog Lilly run free in the open space. Emilio looked over his shoulder at me and said, "Come here. Look what Lilly found, of all things."

To my surprise, it was a pacifier.

Then, when we got home Lilly led us to the baby's room and would not budge.

Our whole marriage we have only had dogs as our "kids", and they don't say a whole lot, so having a baby will be quite a change.

Speaking of change, a little secret that only a few dear friends know is that I've never changed a diaper in my life. Emilio has though. I pray for dear Emilio; he will be a busy man.

The steadfast of mind You will keep in perfect peace, Because he trusts in You.

Isaiah 26:3

❧ WAIT ☙

Yet those who wait for the LORD Will gain new strength...

Isaiah 40:31a

*D*ECEMBER 7, 2018

I was the type of person before having children that thought breastfeeding was strange and not for me. Even when I was expecting Eden, I could not imagine feeding my baby in that way. I would cry over the very thought of having to nurse her.

But after Eden was born it changed everything, and I found myself never wanting to take my eyes off her and could not imagine not nursing her. However, it wasn't a walk in the park and did not come easy for me as I battled a meager milk supply; it was a real struggle. I lost sleep over it. I cried over it many days and nights.

But God in His sovereignty made it possible for me to be able to nurse, even to this day of Eden being almost 2 years old (Psalm 22:9, Isa 49:15).

There are many joys in motherhood and never did I expect breastfeeding to be one of them. I think of Proverbs 16:9 that says, and I paraphrase, a man makes his plans, but the Lord directs his steps, which includes nursing.

My neighbor to right of me is from India and tells me that her mom nursed her till she was five and that she loved her mom very much. How special.

Let's wait on the Lord today. His ways are higher than ours. Submit to Him all your ways (even when you feel your way is right, submit and wait on Him). He will make things clear. In His time. In His way.

Yet those who wait for the LORD Will gain new strength...

Isaiah 40:31a

❧ COMFORT ☙

Let everything that has breath praise the LORD. Praise the LORD!

Psalm 150:6

*D*ECEMBER 8, 2018

It's crazy to me that Eden, being not yet two years old, hardly cries anymore. Instead, she makes all her dolls and stuffed animals cry, and even wants me to pretend to cry so that she can comfort and console me. Perhaps even she is shocked at her lack of crying.

Maybe when we get to heaven it will be the same for us. After all, the Bible says, "He will wipe away every tear from their eyes; and there will no longer be any death; there will no longer be any mourning, or crying, or pain; the first things have passed away." (Revelation 21:4)

What a fine day that will be.

Let everything that has breath praise the LORD. Praise the LORD!

Psalm 150:6

❧ EMOTIONS ☙

The Lord is my portion…

Psalm 119:57a

---

*D*ECEMBER 13, 2018

Michelle, a sister in our church, sent a wonderful text to me an hour before the clock would strike midnight and Eden would turn 2 years old.

I feel good at the moment, and I'm exceedingly grateful as I reflect on all that God has done over the past two years, namely, that He let me live. I almost died after my natural childbirth because of excessive blood loss. But to say that the last two years have been easy is not true. It's been a hard two years. Very hard, actually, and emotionally draining. Not because I haven't wanted to care for Eden but because it's hard to think of these oh so precious moments ending. The thought of Eden getting saved and being forever with me in eternity helps to ease the pain.

There are many things about motherhood that I did not expect, and one of them is that it can be a rollercoaster. Going from rejoicing to weeping to disciplining in the span of a few minutes is something I did not see coming and was at first overwhelmed with.

But the more I found my anchor in the Lord, the less moved I became, which was the very reminder found in a writing by GraceGems.org that Michelle sent to me. Here it is:

If God is my portion, then I ought to be content without any other portion. He is . . . enough in poverty, enough in persecution, enough in life, enough in death, enough for evermore!

If God gives me Himself-then it is more than as if He had given me the whole world, or ten thousand worlds like this! O how happy was the apostle Paul, who knowing God to be his portion could say, 'I have learned to be content whatever the circumstances. I know what it is to be in need, and I know what it is to have plenty. I have learned the secret of being content in any and every situation, whether well fed or hungry, whether living in plenty or in need!' Philippians 4:11-12

If God is my portion, I ought to be thankful. It is enough. There is no losing it. What dignity, what honor is conferred on the man who has God for his portion! I deserved to be stripped of everything, and to be turned out of God's presence eternally penniless, wretched, and miserable. But instead of this, God in His free grace, in His infinite mercy-gives me . . . a heavenly mansion, a glorious city, an eternal kingdom, more, He gives me Himself! God in all His glory, in all His grace-is mine!

If God is my portion, then I ought to be living upon Him. If I live upon anything outside of God, then I live upon what is finite and will change. But if I live upon God, I live upon the infinite, and upon what is unchangeable. As a believer, I should live befitting the dignity of my lofty character, position, and prospects. The man of fortune ought not to live like the pauper.

Just so, the Christian ought to live above other men.

If God is my portion, I ought to be making a proper use of it. I should set my portion over and against . . . all my pains and privations, all my griefs and grievances, all my sadnesses and sorrows.

I should look above all my trials and troubles–and rejoice that throughout eternity, I shall have . . . eternal ease–instead of pain, eternal plenty–instead of privation, eternal joy–instead of grief, eternal gladness–instead of sadness, and eternal bliss–instead of sorrow!

Beloved, is the Lord your portion? Are you living upon Him as such?

But if God is not your portion–then what is? Where are your thoughts most? Where do your affections center? After what do you pursue? The world? It is a poor, fleeting, unsatisfying portion! It will be found insufficient, unsatisfactory, and perishing!

Unless God is your portion, you will be . . . unsatisfied in life, wretched in death, and indescribably miserable to all eternity!

'My flesh and my heart may fail, but God is the strength of my heart and my portion forever!' James Smith, Gleams of Grace 1860"

I'm very thankful that Michelle sent this Grace Gem to me as it got me to thinking. God gives us "things," if you will, in heaven, such as a city, a banqueting table, a room, and golden streets.

But all of that is nothing if He is not there.

It would be as if He gave us the most beautiful home, decorated in the exact style you love and he places you in it to enjoy but you are all by yourself. How miserable that would be. God created us to share life and things with people. As is heaven. It is meant to be shared with the Living God.

Imagine your child goes shopping with your credit card and buys all sorts of things, but then comes home unsatisfied because all they really wanted was time with you. All the gifts in the world mean nothing if the gift giver isn't present. And God is so kind as to give us *all* of Him. What a thought!

How convicting is this quote by James Smith, "If God is my portion, then I ought to be living upon Him. If I live upon anything outside of God-then I live upon what is finite, and will change. But if I live upon God, I live upon the infinite, and upon what is unchangeable."

How easily I am moved!

Let me pray for us this night...

Lord, we realize our need for You more than ever before. We knew we needed You when we got saved, but now more than ever we know our need is real. Help every lady reading this to drink from the Fountain of Living Water. To daily go to the Fountain for a fresh drink. To stop and breathe and wait on You. Forgive us for going to broken cisterns that cannot satisfy. You are our portion. Amen.

Note: I heartily recommend that every one of you dear readers subscribe to Grace Gems Daily Devotional (gracegems.org). The brother that runs Grace Gems emailed to each of his subscribers my husband's film, **UnpopularTheMovie.com**, causing it to receive the most traction it had ever seen. He also posted our film on Sermon Audio, helping it to move quickly to the #1 slot. We are very thankful for all his labor in the Lord.

The Lord is my portion...

Psalm 119:57a

⪼ PRAYER ⪻

Now to Him who is able to do far more abundantly beyond all that we ask or think, according to the power that works within us, to Him be the glory in the church and in Christ Jesus to all generations forever and ever. Amen.

Ephesians 3:20

---

*D*ECEMBER 14, 2018 (2:50am)

It's Eden's 2 Year Birthday!

Praise be to God that I lived to see this day.

This week Eden (while we were on the bed waking from a nap) crawled over and hugged me all on her own. Lord, please put this on her heart to do this more often. Please allow me to see Eden get saved very young. And let it happen with me, if it would please You. Why?

Well here are my few reasons of why I would love to be able to see her get saved in my presence.

1. You put it in my heart to even request this, Lord.

2. I'm asking You by faith.

3. You are faithful and able (this is not too hard for you).

4. It would make my joy full. Truly full.

5. I'm older and would like this joy to help carry me (in my elder days).

6. So our home can be in one accord.

7. Because this was Pastor Chuck Smith's testimony (the pastor of Calvary Chapel and the one who baptized Emilio over 20 years ago) and if you did it for his mom you can with me. He got saved at age 4 with his mom reading him the Bible in his crib. What a testimony. I would love for Eden to say something similar.

8. Because I'm up at 3:00am losing sleep in order to submit it this burden to You.

9. Because in the past I've asked You for things that seemed impossible and you did above and beyond.

Some of you reading this might think I'm crazy in listing things out to the Lord but I have been doing this for years in my personal journals and then I stumbled upon a book by Charles Spurgeon called "The Power in Prayer" where he talks about doing this very thing and being very specific with the Lord. So why don't you take the time to get out a journal or something to write on and give the Lord your care, your worry, your desire or your heart's burden.

Ephesians 3:20-21 says, "Now unto Him who is able to do exceedingly abundantly above all we can ask think or imagine." Since You are able to do above all I can ask or think that means you can do this. This request is nothing for you.

Later that morning I received from a friend this "birthday gift" for Eden:

"My gift to Eden is a prayer...'Oh Lord I thank you for Eden who you created for Your good pleasure. Please give her understanding of her need for You that surpasses the usual 2-year-old mind. I think and wonder how Jesus acted at 2 and want that for Eden as much as is possible for a little sinner. When Eden fails and has a tantrum may Trish remember this prayer that kept 10 more tantrums just like it from happening :-) Amen.

P.S. Trish, you've probably already noticed this, but the 2s are the age of her wanting to do things on her own, which is all practice for receiving Christ on her own. Everything we do in life points to Him and why we need him. Eat, sleep, dress...as you let her do/prepare for all those things tell her why they're necessary and that Jesus is the fulfillment of them all. Which I know you already do, so good job. Praise God for the twos! Love you."

Struggles and Sunshine is a confession book of sorts, so I must confess that I didn't like the first part of that P.S. very much. The part where Eden wants to do things on her own makes me sad. Like John Newton says in the quote below:

> I am not the man I ought to be,
> I am not the man I wish to be,
> I am not the man I hope to be,
> but by the grace of God,
> I am not what I used to be.
>
> **–John Newton**

Now to Him who is able to do far more abundantly beyond all that we ask or think, according to the power that works within us, to Him be the glory in the church and in Christ Jesus to all generations forever and ever. Amen.

Ephesians 3:20

❧ NEXT ❧

---

*Do you not know that those who run in a race all run, but
only one receives the prize?
Run in such a way that you may win.*

1 Corinthians 9:24

DECEMBER 16, 2018

Tonight a picture of Eden in the hospital (the day she
was born) popped up on my Facebook "memories," and
with just one glance I was brought to my knees sobbing.
Time has passed so quickly, and I wish I could do the past
two years all over again.

So, I asked God for another child. Which is funny because I'm 41. I need a miracle.

That won't solve the pain I feel though, and possibly
would only double it (and double the love, no doubt.)

I'm sure you know what I mean.

I think sometimes we (I) need to beware of pictures
that make us look back, when God is calling us to move
forward.

In fact, Paul in Philippians 3:13 says that he "forgets
what lies behind and reaches to what lies ahead." Several
other versions communicate the idea of straining forward,
as if it is extremely hard to do.

It's so easy to look back and stay there and get caught up in thoughts of "if only I had done this differently" or "if only I had more time" or "if only I could do it all over again."

Maybe you don't battle those thoughts, but I often find myself looking back when I need to press, strain, look and reach forward for anything other than my depressed state of mind.

If you've read or listened to the precious saint, Elisabeth Elliot, you have heard her use the phrase "Do the next thing." Here she explains the meaning behind the phrase that has personally carried me many weary days. This is part of a transcript from her Gateway to Joy radio program:

"When I went back to my jungle station after the death of my first husband, Jim Elliot, I was faced with many confusions and uncertainties. I had a good many new roles, besides that of being a single parent and a widow. I was alone on a jungle station that Jim and I had manned together. I had to learn to do all kinds of things, which I was not trained or prepared in any way to do. It was a great help to me simply to do the next thing.

Have you had the experience of feeling as if you've got far too many burdens to bear, far too many people to take care of, far too many things on your list to do? You just can't possibly do it, and you get in a panic, and you just want to sit down and collapse in a pile and feel sorry for yourself.

Well, I've felt that way a good many times in my life, and I go back over and over again to an old Saxon legend, which I'm told is carved in an old English parson somewhere by the sea. I don't know where this is, but this is a poem which was written about that legend. The legend is "Do the next thing." And it's spelled in

*what I suppose is Saxon spelling. "D-O-E for "do,"
"the" "next" "T-H-Y-N-G-E." for "thing."*

*The poem says, 'Do it immediately, do it with prayer,
do it reliantly, casting all care. Do it with reverence,
tracing His hand who placed it before thee with ear-
nest command. Stayed on Omnipotence, safe 'neath
His wing, leave all resultings, do the next thing.'*

*That is a wonderfully saving truth. Just do the next
thing."*

She then explains she would apply this in her missionary work, and then asks the listener,

*"What is the next thing for you to do? Small duties,
perhaps? Jobs that nobody will notice as long as you
do them? A dirty job that you would get out of if you
could have your own preferences? Are you asked to take
some great responsibility, which you really don't feel
qualified to do? You don't have to do the whole thing
right this minute, do you? I can tell you one thing that
you do have to do right this minute. It's the one thing
that is required of all of us every minute of every day.
Trust in the living God."*

*Now, what is the next thing? Well, perhaps it's to get
yourself organized. Maybe you need to clean off your
desk if you have a desk job that needs to be done. Maybe you need to clean out your kitchen drawers if you're
going to do your kitchen work more efficiently. Maybe
you need to organize the children's clothes."*

At one point in her life, Elisabeth Elliot cared for her
grandchildren for a few days and finding the constant de-
mands and needs of several children was overwhelming to
her. When she asked her daughter how she did it all while
nursing a baby, her daughter laughed and said,

*"Well, Mama, I'll tell you how. I do what you told me
years ago to do. Do the next thing. Don't sit down and*

think of all the things you have to do. That will kill you. It's overwhelming. It's daunting if you think of all the things that are involved in a task. Just pick up the next thing."

Elisabeth Elliot's advice is truly wonderful medicine for the weary soul and body.

Proverbs 16:24 says...

"Pleasant words are like a honeycomb,
Sweetness to the soul and health to the bones."

Amen and amen.

---

*Do you not know that those who run in a race all run, but only one receives the prize?
Run in such a way that you may win.*

1 Corinthians 9:24

✣ GIFTS ✣

*D*ECEMBER 17, 2018

Eden has a special cubby in our kitchen. When she is asleep, I clean it out and organize new goodies for her all the while thinking of John 14:3 where Jesus says that He goes to "prepare a place" for us.

Eden never has a clue what I'm up to, which makes me all the more eager to do it. She gets so excited to see what new things the cubby holds, and I'm equally as excited to see her face when she opens it the next day.

I often wonder if the Lord is excited to see our expressions when He reveals special gifts to us.

And can you imagine the excitement that is building in His heart for *the* day when we see Him face-to-face, and He reveals what He has been planning all this time?

How blessed is the one whom You choose and bring near to you; to dwell in your courts...

Psalm 65:4a

❧ IMITATE ❧

You are good and do good; Teach me Your statutes.

Psalm 119:68

*D*ECEMBER 21, 2018

Eden has been sick for five days, and today she has been irritable, which is not like her. Emilio is on the verge of getting sick, and I've been gargling with coconut oil all week to try to kill a sore throat. I just sit with Eden while she naps and gargle away.

I'm really writing because it's one of those days where everything seems off. My family may not know it, but the inside of my heart has been down, tempting me to sulk. This day has proven to be a good reminder of how I need God's grace more and more.

During the day, a friend sent me these two quotes:

"Depression is the opposite end of the same stick of pride."

"The remedy for both depression and pride is to look away from yourself and onto Jesus Christ."

Oh, how I needed those gracious words at that very hour!

And then Eden sang this entire song to me:

"Hark! The herald angels sing,

'Glory to the newborn King!

Peace on earth, and mercy mild,

God and sinners reconciled.'

Joyful, all ye nations, rise,

Join the triumph of the skies;

With th' angelic host proclaim,

'Christ is born in Bethlehem.'

Hark! The herald angels sing,

'Glory to the new-born King!"

Her singing always lifts me. It's been one week since she turned 2, and her growth in terms of knowledge is happening so fast I can hardly keep up. I can only hope my holiness and sanctification is growing like that.

At one point, Eden was playing so gently with her baby she calls "Happy." I watched her cuddle her baby, kiss her about 10 times over and over, and check her temperature to make sure she "felt fine." She was imitating everything I had done to her when she was sick, which made me think of the verse where Paul says, "Imitate me as I imitate Christ."

Now if only she would kiss me ten times instead of her baby!

Philippians 3:17 says, "Join one another in following my example, brothers, and carefully observe those who live according to the pattern we set for you." Children have the "carefully observing" part down, and it seems to me that we never really lose that, which is why Paul gives us that reminder. May God help all of us to observe His Word, and put it carefully into practice. Psalm 119:31 says, "I cling to Your testimonies, O LORD; let me not be put to shame."

As I was changing Eden's diaper, she again started singing "Hark! The Herald Angels Sing." I needed this sweet gift of her voice and the hope of the words.

Lord, as the song says, "glory to the new born King". May He help us fight the good fight of faith. Keep the enemy from devouring our faith. And I pray for those that feel particularly weak, remind them You are strong. You kindly reminded me of just that earlier today when I prayed You would do something wonderful in spite of my sin and off day, and You did through Eden. Bless my sisters reading this. Bless their souls and strengthen their hearts and minds. Glory to the King! In Christ's name, Amen.

You are good and do good; Teach me Your statutes.

Psalm 119:68

ꙩ COME ꙩ

Search me, O God, and know my heart; Try me and know my anxious thoughts!

Psalm 139:23

*D*ECEMBER 23, 2018

"Come unto me, all ye that labour and are heavy laden, and I will give you rest." (Matthew 11:28) This is quite the verse for me today. The part of it that strikes me most is the first three words. Jesus doesn't tell us to go to a biblical counselor (though that can be a blessing at times) nor does He say for you to phone a friend (though there may be a time for that too), instead He wants me (and you) to come to Him.

Perhaps you want to pour out your heart to your husband in hopes of receiving a hug and some nourishing words for your weary soul. But he just doesn't have the patience or care or the right words (most likely because he used all his words for the day already, and you want to go into a story, as I do, at 1:00 in the morning).

The truth is, anyone besides the Lord at times can be like a broken cistern. You go to them, but they can't meet your need; their words just don't do the job. They can't touch you the way the King can. No one knows you as He does. Psalm 139:2 tells us, "You know when I sit down and when I rise up; You understand my thought from afar." It is encouraging (deeply) that He understands our every thought.

The Pulpit Commentary gives more insight into Psalm 139:2 and says: "Thou knowest my downsitting and mine uprising. All that I do from one end of the day to the other. Thou understandest my thought afar off; i.e., while it is just forming - long before it is a fully developed thought."

Sort of sounds like a baby in the womb doesn't it? Long before the child is fully developed, while the child is still forming, God knows all about them. And the same with our thoughts. Long before we have even processed them into a worry, God knows the thought from afar. What a comfort.

If you find yourself (like I do) meditating on your failures or the failures of others for far too long, that is an indicator that something is probably off in your heart. Perhaps a root of bitterness is growing. We must ask the Lord to remove it, as He is the master gardener and will use the proper tool to get it out. Let's purpose to meditate on Him and His word. After all, *He thinks of you* more than anyone does.

Search me, O God, and know my heart; Try me and know my anxious thoughts!

Psalm 139:23

❧ INVITATION ❧

*To Him who sits on the throne, and to the Lamb, be praise
and honor and glory and power
forever and ever!*

Revelation 5:13b

*D*ECEMBER 27, 2018

I've been talking to Eden a lot about the banqueting table, and the marriage supper of the Lamb. She looked deep in my eyes when I said, "I have asked The Lord to sit next to you. There's going to be a big table in heaven, bigger than ours even. And guess who will be serving us food? The Lord. He will probably come up to you and say, 'What can I serve you? What would you like to eat?'"

I told her that she will gladly say, "Oh Lord, I'll eat anything you make me. Anything you make will be delicious!" Her eyes widened as if to say "Tell me more!"

"Blessed are those who are invited to the marriage supper of the Lamb" (Revelation 19:9). May all the dear children (of my beloved readers) be invited to this great supper.

*To Him who sits on the throne, and to the Lamb, be praise
and honor and glory and power
forever and ever!*

Revelation 5:13b

❧ DISTRACTED ❧

Your word I have treasured in my heart,
That I may not sin against You.

Psalm 119:11

*D*ECEMBER 28, 2018

I started teaching Eden Spanish words this week, starting with how to say hair, eyes, nose, mouth, and feet. We talked about playing the guitar and praising God with our hands. She learned very quickly.

Right after our lesson, I was talking to her grandparents on the phone. She began yelling, "I am learning Spanish!" She shouted it about five times. Part of the reason she was acting this way was that I had been on the phone for too long and she wanted my attention.

How often are we distracted when God wants our full attention? Perhaps today, just sit and read the Bible. Even if there is only time to read one verse, meditate on that one, and give thanks.

Your word I have treasured in my heart,
That I may not sin against You.

Psalm 119:11

❧ THANKS ❧

…in everything give thanks; for this is God's will for you in Christ Jesus.

1 Thessalonians 5:18

*J*ANUARY 1, 2019

I received a touching New Year's gift from Eden today. During bath time, she began rubbing my arm and saying, "Thank you, Lord." She did it a few times before it dawned on me what she was saying, so I asked, "What are you thanking God for?" She said, "For Mama's arm." I wonder if I have ever thanked God for my mom's arm? What a simple and profound thanks to Him.

Why don't we take the time today to thank Him for all the different arms that have assisted us in this life. It's quite humbling to do so. Instead of complaining about the arms serving us (which can be so easy), let's thank Him.

…in everything give thanks; for this is God's will for you in Christ Jesus.

1 Thessalonians 5:18

⊱ PROVIDENCE ⊰

My times are in Your hand; Deliver me from the hand of my enemies and from those who persecute me.

Psalm 31:15

*J*ANUARY 2, 2019

A dear sister in our church who suffers from heart rhythm issues sent this to me:

"Firmly believing that my times are in God's hand, I here submit myself and all my affairs for the ensuing year, to the wise and gracious disposal of God's divine providence. Whether God appoints for me health or sickness, peace or trouble, comforts or crosses, life or death— may His holy will be done!" -Matthew Henry

I must admit that Matthew Henry was more godly than I, because I do want to feel good. It can really be hard to enjoy the day when your body is a constant battle (like mine is, not every day, but a lot of the days) but having a constant thorn in the flesh does help you to press into the Lord.

What ever your battle is today, dear sister, let's press into the Lord together. Let's choose to set our minds on Him. To put on a worship song and wage war against our enemies. God will help us. He is stronger than all our foes.

✏ SING ✏

Praise the LORD! For it is good to sing praises to our God...

Psalm 147:1a

*J*ANUARY 3, 2019

A 3:00am thought. Today, Eden quoted almost the entire Greek alphabet through song. My mind was blown. I thought, "Did she really just sing that?"

Singing is a powerful tool though. I did ministry at a convalescent home many years ago where a resident there, a lady of about 90 years of age, could not recall hardly any details of her life. Even the names of her children and her husband escaped her memory, but she knew the tune and words to Christian songs. It was truly amazing. I can't stress enough that if you have little ones to implement singing as a way of teaching.

I was joking with Eden the day I told her I was going to teach her the Greek and Hebrew alphabet. I began singing thinking she wasn't going to be into it very much, but boy, was I wrong.

When I got to one letter in the Greek alphabet that is pronounced "oops-a-lon" she lost it laughing. She said, "Mama again!" and "Oops, oops, oops, a-lon!!!" I'm definitely going to keep singing to her. After all, God invented singing. Just read Zephaniah 3:16-17 (ESV), and then think about God singing over you, if you can even imagine it.

The thought of God singing is far too much and too special for my little mind to try to grasp, let alone to think of Him singing *over me*. I vividly remember my mom singing over me, from a very young age (like 2 years old... don't laugh, but I really do have snapshots in my mind of it). God allows us to sing over our little children so we can get a glimpse of how He feels when He sings over us. Wow!

Praise the LORD! For it is good to sing praises to our God...

Psalm 147:1a

❧ GRATITUDE ☙

*J*ANUARY 3, 2019 (another early morning thought...)

Eden woke up this morning and instantly looked at the new blanket Emilio had put on her after she had fallen asleep last night. She said in the most adorable voice, "Thank you, Mama, for this blanket." Do you know those six little words carried me all day? Even though I wasn't the one that had put the blanket on her, it just amazed me that she recognized it was given to her during the night to keep her warm. She was grateful for such a small thing.

God continually gives us blankets, if you will. In fact, we read in Lamentations 3:23 that His mercies are "new every morning." When was the last time you thanked God for your nightly blanket? I'm asking myself the same question and am totally convicted by it.

And think about how often words can carry us as Eden's did me. God gave us a giant book of His words for precisely the same reason; allow them to carry your willing or weary soul today.

For thou wilt light my candle: the LORD my God will enlighten my darkness.

Psalm 18:28

❧ GOOD ☙

…She laughs at the time to come.

Proverbs 31:25b ESV

*J*ANUARY 3, 2019 (another entry, sleeplessness.)

I took Eden to the library today. A Muslim mom was there with two boys that were not well behaved. I felt bad for all three of them.

The older one, who was maybe 6 years old, threw one of the worst tantrums I've ever seen in public. Eden looked mortified. I said, "That dear boy probably needs a nap. Let's pray for him."

When we got home with our (about 20) library books I was still burdened for the family and prayed more. I was holding Eden in my bathroom, while putting her for a nap, when she said, "God is good to me." I said, "Yes Edie Joy, He is."

The night before she told me, "Mama, God is not mean. God is good." Amen to that.

After the library, Eden was reading her illustrated children's Bible. She was looking at the pictures and started listing off those she recognized. "David, Goliath, Queen Esther…" Then she looked at the little tomb with the stone rolled away, took her little finger and pointed and said, "That's where Jesus got hurt." It's hard for me to even write this without weeping. I have not talked much to her lately about the tomb and what happened to our King, but apparently, she is beginning to piece things together. I'm thankful to live to see that.

Later in the day Eden told me, "I love Mama's tummy."

"That used to be your home," I said.

That I even uttered those words is surreal since I used to have no interest in having kids...as in zero interest. But God changes the heart; it's His specialty. He likes to take dark hearts and make them shine. His delight is to take unkempt places and make them spotless.

I used to think the verse about children being a "heritage from the Lord" was for other people. How blind I was! I thank God for opening my eyes before it was too late. I'm 41 as I write this, and I have a two-year-old. Did I just write that?

If God was able to help Sarah and Abraham in their old age, He can help all of us. Let's present our requests to God, and let His peace that surpasses all understanding guard our hearts and minds in Christ Jesus.

I'm sure many of you reading this fear (as I do) the type of world our precious children will grow up in. Let's really try to take this verse to heart...

...She laughs at the time to come.

Proverbs 31:25b ESV

❧ FORWARD ☙

Let us press on to know the LORD.

Hosea 6:3

*J*ANUARY 4, 2019

Meditating on the Bible, working on this book, and studying for the Real Estate exam have kept my mind busy leaving little time (thankfully) for me to mull over my woes.

Psalm 127:1-2 says, "Unless the Lord builds the house, the builders labor in vain. Unless the Lord watches over the city, the guards stand watch in vain. In vain you rise early and stay up late, toiling for food to eat—for he grants sleep to those he loves."

I must confess, I am deeply prone to mulling over my woes, and looking at the past for things I should have handled differently, while simultaneously beating myself up for wasted time. I must remember Jesus' warning in Luke 9:62 that says, "No one who puts his hand to the plow and looks back is fit for the kingdom of God." God has us moving forward to bring about His purpose. So, keep pressing forward dear ones, and I will too.

Let us press on to know the LORD.

Hosea 6:3

❧ MERCY ❧

The LORD is gracious and merciful; Slow to anger and great in lovingkindness.

Psalm 145:8

*J*ANUARY 7, 2019

Today, Eden dug up an old wallet-sized picture of me from my junior year of high school. I was dressed in a fancy gown with a crown on my head, and was standing next to four other girls. She said, "There is mama and girls going to church." This was so precious to hear, but if only it were true. I would have much rather that we had been going to church than attending a worldly event. The picture reminded me of one glorious truth though; it was taken around the time that God opened my eyes to my sin and my need for Him. Praise God for that. I pray that Eden Joy will get saved at the earliest age possible and escape toddler sin, junior high sin, college sin and so much more sin. It is possible. My friend James White was saved as a child and is still walking with the Lord to this day. His ministry reaches many with the truths of the Gospel. I have talked to the Lord often about James' testimony and how it would be wonderful if He would do the same thing for Eden.

A late night thought: There are reasons why I'm not crazy about Facebook, even though I am on there. Tonight, for instance, I logged in and read about a little girl who is Eden's age (2) and is dying of cancer. Apparently, the doctors can't do anything to remove the cancerous tumor because it will kill her. At that point, I had to stop reading.

I don't even know these people, but their sad story popped up on my News Feed. I'm so broken for them. Especially because they appear spiritually lost. The curse words the mom wrote in her post amidst her suffering was difficult to read. I stopped and prayed this for them: Lord, the pain people are experiencing in this world is too much for us to handle. But not for You. You know pain very, very well. So, would you comfort this family in the way that you know best? Draw them to yourself. Please, Lord. And bring that child safe to your heavenly kingdom. Lord, I want to confess all my sin to you...all my complaining, all my coveting, all my dissatisfaction with the lot you've given me. Please forgive me, dear King. Please wash me. I think of Isaiah in chapter 6 where he talks about being unclean and amongst an unclean people, and he needed You to take coal to cleanse his lips. Please be gracious to me Lord, and maybe use something less drastic than a lump of coal, because that sounds terribly painful. Cleanse your people and have mercy. In Christ's name, Amen.

The LORD is gracious and merciful; Slow to anger and great in lovingkindness.

Psalm 145:8

❧ BATTLE ❧

The LORD will save me, and we will play my music on stringed instruments all the days of our lives, at the house of the LORD.

Isaiah 38:20

*J*ANUARY 8, 2019

Spurgeon said, "I have learned to kiss the waves that throw me against the Rock of Ages."

I must admit...I fail to do this a lot. Like today, for example.

Nothing went wrong per se; it's just been a battle of the mind. Because of that, I was reminded to daily purpose to "put on the full armor of God" (Ephesians 6:10-17) and to speak godly truth to myself. I think as moms we have to be especially on guard spiritually because we are giving ourselves non-stop and don't particularly have a lot of time to fuel up on God's Word. And if we're lacking in our time in His Word, we become spiritually weak.

What I try to do with Eden is to incorporate Scripture songs throughout the day that can wash us both.

Putting on worship music in the car, in the house, or on a walk, dispels the darkness and lifts downcast hearts.

And if you are like me, you might need to listen to the same worship song over and over until the darkness lifts. But it will!

We must open the Word of God, believe and quote it as Jesus did in Matthew 4 during deep temptation. Jesus did not fight with any other weapon other than Scripture, which amazes me. He only used words.

Quoting Scripture through song or singing biblical truth only stands to strengthen us and be a balm to a weary soul. To get you started, I have included a list of worship songs, mostly geared towards kids, in the Worshiping God chapter of this book. Sing Praise!

The LORD will save me, and we will play my music on stringed instruments all the days of our lives, at the house of the LORD.

Isaiah 38:20

❧ FAITHFUL ❧

Weeping may last for the night, But a shout of joy comes in the morning.

Psalm 30:5

JANUARY 16, 2019

Do you ever feel like a Gomer? You know the woman Hosea took as a wife that was continually unfaithful to him? Yet through it all, Hosea never left her, but instead, remained faithful.

What Hosea did is a picture of Christ and the Church. Christ calls His people, meaning He calls the stained ones, the dirty ones, the ones in need of Him, and cleaned us up. Even after our salvation, He continues to do a profound work of pruning out the Gomer-like idolatries within us. You may not constantly be committing actual adultery like Gomer, but what adulteries are in your heart?

I'm the first to admit, I have to guard my heart with Eden, and fail at doing a good job of it. I tend to get sad if she doesn't greet me like she does others. Or if she runs to her Papa instead of me while we are out at a store. People will say, "Well she is with you all the time" and that's true, but it still hurts. And Emilio handles it so much better than I do. He doesn't seem to get bothered with her going throughout the house, always calling for me. But for me, when she starts showing too much attention to others, I can get bothered (not all the time but it can hit me out of the blue).

Perhaps that is how the Lord feels when we give too much of our lives to another. There must be a balance, which sometimes there is with me, but I want to be consistently upright in the inward parts before Him like the Psalmist speaks of in 51:6, "Behold, You desire truth in the innermost being, and in the hidden part You will make me know wisdom." I confessed my jealously (really greed, because I think I deserve more or better), to a friend in California, and I was shocked to hear that she battles the same thing. Up to now, I felt alone in my sin. Isn't sin always that way? You think no one else struggles as you do, and therefore, you are ashamed to confess it causing it to breed more.

But let's heed the words of James about confessing and praying for one another: "Therefore, confess your sins to one another, and pray for one another so that you may be healed. The effective prayer of a righteous man can accomplish much." (James 5:16) I confessed this sin of jealously/greed to my mom to which she, in turn, asked for prayer for similar things and sent me Philippians 4:6-7 and Ephesians 6:12, which helped tremendously. I know it's important to not confess to the world (like I might be doing right now, ha!), but to trustworthy sisters or your mom (especially if she is saved). I write this in hopes that any of you going through similar things will not feel alone, but instead will be encouraged to fight your sin.

I remember a missionary friend who once came to our house with her 2-year-old son. She was deeply depressed over the fact that her son greeted his daddy so happily, only to act like she didn't exist. I have no idea how I comforted her at the time. I was probably inwardly just praying it wouldn't happen to me. I got to thinking the other day that the role of a mom is much like the Holy

Spirit. The Holy Spirit does so much and yet gets so neglected. He convicts us, cleans us up, comforts us, helps us and instructs us. Sounds a lot like a mom. Yet we forget to offer much praise or thanks to Him.

In John 14:16 Jesus said... *"I will ask the Father, and He will give you another Helper, that He may be with you forever..."* When was the last time you thanked God for your mom and for the Holy Spirit? I'm thankful I have the Spirit to convict me of my wretchedness and that He won't leave me this way. I'm thankful I have a mom to send me Scripture verses to encourage and sharpen me. Praise God! Paul said in Philippians 1:6, " For I am confident of this very thing, that He who began a good work in you will perfect it until the day of Christ Jesus."

J.C. Ryle said, "Let us take comfort in the thought that the Lord Jesus does not cast off His believing people because of failures and imperfections. He knows what they are. He takes them, as the husband takes the wife, with all their blemishes and defects, and once joined to Him by faith, will never leave them. He is a merciful and compassionate High-priest. It is His glory to pass over the transgressions of His people and to cover their many sins. He knew what they were before conversion–wicked, guilty, and defiled; yet He loved them. He knows what they will be after conversion–weak, erring, and frail; yet He loves them. He has undertaken to save them, notwithstanding all their shortcomings, and what He has undertaken He will perform."

Here is my prayer for us...Lord you know our hearts, and you are able to conquer them. Thank you for the work you started. That means it is not done. It is only beginning. And that can be painful and hard at times, but we ask that You would give us grace as You dig deeper to make us brilliant like a diamond. We confess our need of You, and that we are weak. But You are strong. Amen."

Side note: Both tears and laughter occurred writing this particular days entry. After I wrote it, I sent it to the sister compiling this book and said, "Tell me what you think of this before putting it in the book." This is our correspondence, starting with her reply:

I love it. You writing this entry is actually an answer to prayer. I thought of Philippians 2:3 after reading the part about Eden running to Emilio. That helps me tremendously when holding too tightly and jealousy rears its head. I sometimes struggle with what you're going thru, just not with my daughter. As far as whether to confess this to the world I thought of Proverbs 11:14. You will have a multitude of counselors after this goes out. Haha :-)

Me: *Ouch. That verse, Philippians 2:3. I think I need to tattoo it on my hand. On Proverbs 11:14. I guess I won't have to worry about Proverbs 11:13...no one will gossip about me because I've aired it all out. Haha!*

Her: *Exactly.*

Her: *Btw, there were two ladies in their Jesus shirts at a red light handing out tracts today. They were heretical, but still was convicting. One had such a thick African accent I literally couldn't understand a single word she said to me. I gave her a Million (tract).*

Me: *Now I almost woke up the baby laughing!*

Praise God for laughter and the prayers of the saints.

Weeping may last for the night, But a shout of joy comes in the morning.

Psalm 30:5

❧ DELIGHT ❧

Therefore if you have been raised up with Christ, keep seeking the things above, where Christ is, seated at the right hand of God. Set your mind on the things above, not on the things that are on earth. For you have died and your life is hidden with Christ in God. When Christ, who is our life, is revealed, then you also will be revealed with Him in glory.

Colossians 3:1-4

*J*ANUARY 18, 2019

I often think of what my future will look like, and pray that Eden will never do to me what I did to my mom, meaning, move away to another state. In my case, it wasn't my choice; I had to follow my husband as the Lord guided him to Texas. Which I was excited to do but leaving California for Texas was terribly hard on me, but was much harder on my mom, and I now understand why. At the time we did not have any children so I couldn't fully comprehend her pain of seeing me drive away into a future without her. It pains me to even type it. Thankfully she now only lives 7 minutes from me and I see her almost daily. And we talk and text a lot. I'm so glad she is alive and in my life. God is kind to have given me someone who cares so much.

And now I find myself getting consumed with the future that I miss true joy right in front of me. I get overwhelmed with what I *may* one day lose instead of enjoying what I *possess* today. Scripture, and the sharpening of the saints have helped me though, especially when I have longed to make time slow down. Like when my friend Kristen told me, "Long to see Christ's face. That will make time drag." Wow. What a thought. I must not long enough for the Lord. In fact, I know I don't. Psalm 37:4 says, *"Delight yourself in the Lord, and he will give you the desires of your heart."* If we are delighting in Him, that means He will provide us with desires in keeping with His will. What a gift!

Another great gift He bestows on us is our children. It's important to remember that they truly belong to God and are merely on loan to us as the guides of their souls. However, if God purposes to save them, then they will be ours for eternity in terms of getting to fellowship together over what matters most, worshiping our King.

Speaking of eternity, I've requested that Eden's room be near my room in heaven, as well as my mom's and all the members of our church. And I've requested Steven Curtis Chapman's room to be near mine too so that I can request songs. His albums were the first to minister to my soul when I got saved in the late 90's. I would sit upstairs in the home my mom and I were living in and get the CD jacket out and plop myself in front of the radio and read every word from his "Speechless" CD. Some of the words I couldn't even see because I was crying so hard. This particular thought of heaven and giving the Lord requests like these may seem silly, but He can fulfill it if He pleases. I believe it's thoughts like these that can help carry us in dark times when days are too short and goodbyes too long.

Soli Deo Gloria!

Therefore if you have been raised up with Christ, keep seeking the things above, where Christ is, seated at the right hand of God. Set your mind on the things above, not on the things that are on earth. For you have died and your life is hidden with Christ in God. When Christ, who is our life, is revealed, then you also will be revealed with Him in glory.

Colossians 3:1-4

❧ REDEMPTION ☙

*Let us not become weary in doing good, for at the proper time we
will reap a harvest if we do not give up.*

Galatians 6:9

*J*ANUARY 19, 2019

Emilio told me recently a story about Kyle Kuzma, a basketball player with the LA Lakers.

He grew up in an impoverished neighborhood in Flint, Michigan raised solely by his mom, and they were very close.

She eventually had to do what many moms dread, which was let her son leave home for college to pursue his basketball dreams. The night before he left, she said she held him and cried, and he did too.

Eventually, letting him go paid off (quite literally). He was drafted 27th by the NBA (which is very low in the draft but still was drafted). He now outscores most of his Lakers teammates and came close to receiving the Rookie Of The Year title. But the beautiful part is he lives in a mansion in Los Angeles *with his mom*.

I started crying in the kitchen as Emilio told me this story of rags to riches. It reminds me so much of salvation. We brought God nothing, and He gave us everything: Himself, redemption, and a heavenly kingdom to look forward to.

I'm sure Kuzma's mom doesn't regret letting him go for those few years. May God reward all of you moms reading this in a wonderful way for all the letting go you have ever had to do.

Let us not become weary in doing good, for at the proper time we will reap a harvest if we do not give up.

Galatians 6:9

❧ SLEEP ❧

...for He gives to his beloved sleep.

Psalm 127:2b

*J*ANUARY 19, 2019

I was asked yesterday, "What if Eden wants to become a doctor?"

I totally understand the question. She has seen quite a few doctors in her short life. She broke her little arm requiring several doctor visits and has been sick on a few occasions where I took her in just to be safe. Because of those visits, she pretends to do x-rays, and checks the heart, lungs, ears, mouth and eyes on whomever and whatever doll or animal is available. I have been thinking a lot about the schooling that is required to be a doctor, and how little I would see her, and it all tends to freak me out. I would be glad for her to help people, but I think I'll pray for others to do that job instead.

I find myself praying about what I would love for her to do (which I hope is God's will), and that is for her to be a mom and to have as many kids as possible (maybe because that is what I wish I would have done looking back on my life). I pray this partially out of selfishness (okay, perhaps mostly) for already wanting grandkids, but I'm sure you understand. I'm turning 42 in April, getting close to the other side of childbearing, which perhaps helps me pray this way too.

I'm reminded of Charles Spurgeon, in his book *The Power of Prayer*, encouraging his readers to make lists to God of reasons why you want Him to answer your prayers and petitions in a specific manner. After giving thanks, here is my list to Him:

1. That Eden would be a mom (only if that's the best for her and is according to Your will)...

2. For my and Emilio's joy (as well as our whole family).

3. Because your Word is true and says children are a blessing (Psalm 127:3-4). Let her heart understand and grasp this early.

4. So she can disciple them (assuming she gets saved, which I should be laboring over in prayer too).

5. Because time is short, and Emilio and I are older.

6. Because your Word calls her to be a keeper at home (something I fought against for years). May Eden be like the women Titus describes:

Titus 2:3-5

"Older women likewise are to be reverent in their behavior, not malicious gossips nor enslaved to much wine, teaching what is good, so that they may encourage the young women to love their husbands, to love their children, to be sensible, pure, workers at home, kind, being subject to their own husbands, so that the Word of God will not be dishonored."

7. Because it will make Eden happy. Psalm 113:9 speaks to that truth in several different versions, all of them wonderful:

"He gives the barren woman a home, making her the joyous mother of children. Praise the LORD!" (ESV)

"He settles the barren woman in her home, as a joyful mother to her children. Hallelujah." (Berean Study Bible)

"He makes the barren woman abide in the house, as a joyful mother of children. Praise the LORD!" (NASB)

"He maketh the barren woman to keep house, and to be a joyful mother of children. Praise ye the LORD." (KJV)

Here are some comforting verses that help me to continue to labor in prayer...

"Ask and it will be given to you; seek and you will find; knock and the door will be opened to you." (Matthew 7:7)

"I sought the LORD, and He answered me; He delivered me from all my fears." (Psalm 34:4)

"Delight yourself in the LORD, and He will give you the desires of your heart." (Psalm 37:4)

"If you then, being evil, know how to give good gifts to your children, how much more will your Father who is in heaven give good things to those who ask Him!" (Matthew 7:11)

I can think of 20 more reasons to labor in prayer, but it's almost 4:00am, so I better go to bed for God says He gives His beloved sleep.

...for He gives to his beloved sleep.

Psalm 127:2b

❧ BROTHER ❧

The LORD will always guide you; He will satisfy you in a sun-scorched land and strengthen your frame. You will be like a well-watered garden, like a spring whose waters never fail.

Isaiah 58:11

*J*ANUARY 23, 2019

Today's Charles Spurgeon Devotion,

"I have exalted one chosen out of the people" (Psalm 89:19.) Why was Christ chosen out of the people? Speak, my heart, for heart-thoughts are best. Was it not that he might be able to be our brother, in the blest tie of kindred blood? Oh, what relationship there is between Christ and the believer! The believer can say, 'I have a Brother in heaven; I may be poor, but I have a Brother who is rich, and is a King, and will he suffer me to want while he is on his throne? Oh, no! He loves me; he is my Brother.' Believer, wear this blessed thought, like a necklace of diamonds, around the neck of thy memory; put it, as a golden ring, on the finger of recollection, and use it as the King's own seal, stamping the petitions of thy faith with confidence of success. He is a brother born for adversity, treat him as such. Christ was also chosen out of the people that he might know our wants and sympathize with us. 'He was tempted in all points like as we are, yet without sin.' In all our sorrows we have his sympathy. Temptation, pain, disappointment, weakness, weariness, poverty; he knows them all, for he has felt all. Remember this, Christian, and let it comfort thee. However difficult and painful thy road, it is marked by the footsteps of thy Saviour; and even when thou reachest the dark valley of the shadow of death and the deep waters of the swelling Jordan, thou wilt find his footprints there. In all places whithersoever we go, he has been our forerunner; each burden we have to carry has once been laid on the shoulders of Immanuel. 'His way was much rougher and darker than mine Did Christ, my Lord, suffer, and shall I repine?'

Take courage! Royal feet have left a blood-red track upon the road, and consecrated the thorny path forever."

The LORD will always guide you; He will satisfy you in a sun-scorched land and strengthen your frame. You will be like a well-watered garden, like a spring whose waters never fail.

Isaiah 58:11

ᚦ GRACE ᚦ

The LORD is near to the brokenhearted And saves those who are crushed in spirit.

Psalm 34:18

---

*F*EBRUARY 1, 2019

I didn't wake up today planning for my day to go the way it did. It started off on a good enough note, then Eden did a few disobedient things such as not wanting to run an errand with me, desiring instead to stay home and play. It's easy to take her defiance personally, like I often do, but I must remember I am training her and I need to lead by example. The truth is, it is easy to forget that.

Eden never knew it, but her disobedience occupied my mind and bothered me for four hours. Isn't that terrible? I could have been and should have been rejoicing in God's goodness, but instead, my heart was stuck in the muck and mire. The Lord is showing me that I'm too quickly moved by a two-year-old. He's reminding me that I should be fixed on the Rock so that I will *not* be moved. He is also showing me that I have unrealistic expectations of Eden being perfect and never sinning. I know this to be true because when Eden sins I'm more offended that it's me she is dishonoring instead of the Lord.

I've decided I must say this to myself 10 times today (maybe every day!), "This isn't about you! Eden's a sinner (so am I). We both need grace and correction and love. Show Eden the right way to handle doing what we don't want to do and that when we're obedient, it honors God. Oh my soul, did you really think she was never going to sin?"

I pray for all of us: Father, forgive me (us) for any wasted time. Somehow redeem it with Romans 8:28. I pray for the dear soul reading this who may have found themselves sulking or having a pity party like the one I had, that You would shine the light of your Word on their soul. Thank you for King David who was often despairing, yet preached truth to himself saying, "Why are you so downcast oh my soul? Hope in God." Amen.

Amid my 4-hour sulking, I called a friend. She's the one who told me that Eden's defiance wasn't about me, and she said this:

"I remember years ago when my daughter was seemingly walking with the Lord, there was great fellowship and then she fell away after her college professor filled her head with nonsense regarding the Bible. That was hurtful that she believed him over me. Ultimately though, it was a rejection of God's Word, not mine. I have to remind myself of that even today, six years later."

I needed to hear that.

After all of this, Eden and I went to my mom's house. I was still a bit down and told her why. When we got home I texted my mom, saying, "Sorry for being down and being so self-centered." She wrote back... "That's ok, we are always here for you when you need to talk. You didn't come across as self-centered, being down can happen to us all. Eden is blessed to have you as a mom. All your training with Eden really shows, your labor has not been in vain; God has been there all along guiding and helping you along the way. And He will continue to be with you on your journey with Eden. 'Anxiety in a man's heart weighs him down, but a good word makes him glad.' Proverbs 12:25"

I needed to hear that too.

Finally, I read what my friend Rachel Zwayne posted on her *Joyful Mothers* Facebook group page. The timing could not have been better:

> *You feel like a failure, You're discouraged and weary and feel like you can't go on. You may not feel like there's fight left in you, but when God is involved, EVERYTHING is possible.*
>
> **"...being confident of this very thing, that He who has begun a good work in you will complete it until the day of Jesus Christ."**
> **Philippians 1:6**

All of the pain from the day washed away when before bed Eden grabbed her little Bible and said, "Let me just read a couple verses."

"Why?" I asked.

She said, "Cubz, Eden loves Jesus."

The LORD is near to the brokenhearted And saves those who are crushed in spirit.

Psalm 34:18

❧ CHANGES ❧

*F*EBRUARY 2, 2019

I sent a quick note to a friend in the Lord saying, "Having a hard day with how fast Eden is growing. You would think I'd be over it. Haha. She is not the same child as last week. Growing so fast. It's hard. Just confessing. Hope you are well. Love you, Trish."

Truth is, I debated over and over whether I should even send the note, but when I received her reply I was glad I did. She said, "Funny that you should text me tonight. I've had a rough few days, too."

She then went on to explain that her daughter is about to be engaged, and while she is happy about the pending engagement, her daughter is absolutely on cloud nine. My friend realized the changes that were about to be brought upon their relationship. She added, "So, with all that being said, I can understand you completely and to be honest, it's nice to know that I'm not alone."

She told me that she had just told her husband that she feels very alone in her feelings because other moms seem to be handling separation from their kids with no problem at all. But for her, the whole thing was so, so hard. She closed by saying, "Anyway, I'm praying for you tonight and am thankful for your friendship. Praise the Lord for His sympathy and love. He remembers that we are dust." I was deeply comforted by this and still am, even as I write.

On a lighter note…before bed, Eden said, "I have to go number 1 and 2 and 3 and 4." I chuckled. Then she added, "Matthew, Mark, Luke, and John." She was trying to say she needed to go potty, but she added a few numbers and also the lyrics to a song we have been memorizing called "Let's Sing The New Testament," which starts off with 1…2…3…4…Matthew, Mark, Luke, and John" God knew I needed the laugh.

Therefore let us draw near with confidence to the throne of grace, so that we may receive mercy and find grace to help in time of need.

Hebrews 4:16

ꙮ TIME ꙮ

Every good thing given and every perfect gift is from above, coming down from the Father of lights, with whom there is no variation or shifting shadow.

James 1:17

*F*EBRUARY 6, 2019

I didn't plan to wake up with a sore throat today, but I did. I told Eden that I had to wear a mask to keep her and Papa from possibly getting sick. I drew a cute happy face on the mask, but she still said, "Mama I do not like it." I told her I understood, and that sometimes we need to do things we do not like.

For instance, I became licensed in real estate yesterday after passing the Real Estate exam even though in all honesty I am not crazy about real estate, neither buying nor selling. My husband sees an opportunity for me though during this season of life, and as long as whatever I do doesn't take much time from Eden and caring for my duties at home, then I'm up for it. Such it is with the mask. I'm not crazy about wearing it, but it serves a useful purpose. I almost forget I'm wearing it at times, like when I was driving in the car today. I bet I was quite the sight.

Another thing I had to do today was join an Association of Realtors and it wasn't cheap. So to redeem the time, while Eden and I were at the office signing up, we passed out some gospel tracts and took advantage of the hour spent there. Eden even got a balloon out of it and said very loudly when we were leaving (while waving it in the air) "Mama bought this for me!"

Maybe this real estate endeavor will be a new small ministry. That is my prayer…that God will redeem all the time spent and use it somehow.

I was reminded this morning of the Proverbs 31 woman who had a husband and children and also "considered a field to buy it." She is perhaps one of the first realtors mentioned in Scripture.

Maybe some of you reading this have to work a job that you are not so crazy about. May God fill you with opportunities to reach others for Christ right where He has you. And may you look for ways to be lighthearted on the job instead of waiting for the job to *end* to really start living.

The most wonderful thing happened after we got home from the Association of Realtors office. Eden and I were outside, she was playing in the grass, I was talking to a neighbor while sitting on our little brick wall, when she suddenly ran over to me, threw her arms around my neck and said, "Mama, I love you." I couldn't believe she did that. Perhaps it was because I had taken off the mask. Maybe I should be sick more often.

Every good thing given and every perfect gift is from above, coming down from the Father of lights, with whom there is no variation or shifting shadow.

James 1:17

❧ ANSWERS ☙

The world is passing away, and also its lusts; but the one who does the will of God lives forever.

1 John 2:17

*F*EBRUARY 7, 2019

Today, I was dreading going to a meeting for realtors because I didn't want to leave Eden at home. I planned it so that the meeting would be while she was sleeping. Thankfully, there are not many mandatory meetings, but this was one was, and it was scheduled to last four hours. I prayed to the Lord to "please use this time. Please do not let it be a waste."

When I walked into the place, I was surprised to see about fifty other realtors, five at each table. I walked around trying to decide where to sit. I think I walked around the room twice, finally choosing the back table. I sat in my chair looking down for about two minutes, looked up, scanned the people at our table and said, "Darlene!?"

There, sitting across from me, was my next-door neighbor from the town Emilio and I moved from. I had not seen Darlene in years; what a huge answer to prayer that I would run into her here. I remember sharing the gospel with her several times and buying her a journal and a Bible. What's funny is our house was for sale during that time, but it just would not sell. In fact, we showed it to prospective buyers 75 times. During that time, Darlene came over to our home to talk about some terrible marital trouble she was having. She cried on my shoulder and I ministered the Lord to her. Emilio did too. Shortly after this, she moved away, and our house finally sold.

While at the training I said a prayer: Father, thank you for this opportunity. Thank you for helping me redeem the time and for answering my prayer with Darlene. Thank you for the Proverbs 31 woman that considered a field and bought it, and from her earnings planted a vineyard. What an encouragement she is. Please use the time that I'm away from Eden to draw us closer, as I would rather be with her than here. Please redeem the time further by allowing this new endeavor to bless our home and our family. Bless the work of my hands. (Ecclesiastes 9:10.) In Christ's name, Amen.

During the training, two Bible verses were quoted during a question and answer session with no Scripture reference: Do unto others as you would have them do to you, and pride comes before the fall. I laughed inside. I don't know if the people that quoted these two verses were Christians, but as Emilio says, "unbelievers live like Christians every day." Praise God for the opportunity to hand out to every person at my table Ray Comfort's tract *Albert Brainstein*, and Unpopular the movie cards. May He use them in a mighty way.

Where ever life finds you today, commit your path to the Lord and try to make the best of it. Remember there are dying souls all around us. Look for ways to bless someone. May He give you strength to rejoice in Him.

The world is passing away, and also its lusts; but the one who does the will of God lives forever.

1 John 2:17

❧ CONFIDENCE ❧

This is the confidence which we have before Him, that, if we ask anything according to His will, He hears us.

1 John 5:17

*F*EBRUARY 8, 2019

A very encouraging word on prayer that I read today:

"All men are able to pray, but only the children of God are able to pray effectively. It is the Holy Spirit that enables you to pray effectively and sincerely, according to the will of God, in the name of Jesus Christ, because it is the Holy Spirit who carries and moves your human spirit to pray fervently, with sincerity, in accordance to the will of God, so that God will hear and answer them. So why are you so moved to pray to God, sincerely begging and desiring for His will to be done? Because the Holy Spirit is carrying your spirit to do so. The Holy Spirit is working upon your soul in such a way that you are like a true son of God, seeing God as a Father, and running to Him, not out of slavish duty, but by the instinct of your new nature. Those moments when you instinctively run to the Lord in times of trouble, immediately crying out for His help without even considering anything else, are by the Spirit of God. You've been adopted, and God is making sure you behave as a child of His, even giving you the impulses toward Him that a child has toward their parents." -Joshua Arnold

---

This is the confidence which we have before Him, that, if we ask anything according to His will, He hears us.

1 John 5:17

☙ TEACHER ❧

As the deer pants for the water brooks, So my soul pants for You, O God.

Psalm 42:1

*F*EBRUARY 13, 2019

I am so easily moved by things. Eden and I had a fun day today, and then before bed, she picked up her baby doll and said, "Look this baby sucks her thumb." I was surprised she said that. I have never taught her about thumb sucking, and have even gone so far as to not mention it because I didn't want her to start the habit. I asked her where she had learned about it, and sure enough, someone had told her.

It bothered me because I monitor her closely yet still had missed out on her learning something. How silly, I know. I even debated whether this was worth anyone's time reading, but the more I thought about it, the more I knew there were biblical lessons that my heart needs to heed that may benefit others as well, such as I'm not the primary teacher in Eden's life, God is.

It should not bother me when she learns from others, as long as they are not unrighteous things. My feelings are a mix of a godly desire of always wanting to be there, which sometimes amounts to greed and pride, and we all know what comes after pride (Proverbs 16:18). I must purpose to rejoice that I have a child that can talk to me and reason, is healthy and growing. (Just after this thumb-sucking incident went down I saw a posting on Facebook about a terribly sick girl not much younger than Eden. Someone I didn't know, but it snapped me instantly back to reality). I also must remember that God wants to be *our* primary teacher and educator just like we want to be with our children. So my heart in this situation is not totally sinful. Whew.

God says, "I will instruct you and teach you in the way you should go; I will counsel you with my eye upon you." (Psalm 32:8) A different rendering says, "I will instruct you and teach you the way you should go; I will give you counsel and watch over you."

God watches over us all the time. He never slumbers or sleeps. We want to watch over our children all the time, which is a good desire, but we must guard that from going south. Psalm 33:18 says, "Surely the eyes of the LORD are on those who fear Him, on those whose hope is in His loving devotion." Psalm 34:11, "Come, children, listen to me; I will teach you the fear of the LORD." Psalm 73:24, "You guide me with Your counsel, and later receive me in glory." Psalm 143:8, "Let me hear Your loving devotion in the morning, for I have put my trust in You. Teach me the way I should walk, for to You I lift up my soul." May those verses minister to you as they do me.

I love so much being able to stay home with Eden as I get to see her learning and growing in front of my eyes. That is such a gracious gift from God. Lord, forgive us for our sins and for our hearts that can turn good things into bad things. Thank you that you remember we are but dust (Psalm 103:14). You know our frame and our weaknesses. Thank you there is forgiveness in You, that You might be feared (Psalm 130:4) Help me Lord not to cry and suck my thumb over this. Amen.

Very thankful for the reminder of this verse that I read before bed.

"You, O Lord, will keep them; you will guard us from this generation forever. On every side the wicked prowl, as vileness is exalted among the children of man." (Psalm 12:7-8)

Thank you, Lord, that you keep us, please guard our hearts against sin, the world, and the schemes of the devil. In Jesus' name. Amen.

As the deer pants for the water brooks, So my soul pants for You, O God.

Psalm 42:1

❧ ENTRUSTED ❧

Thanks be to God for His indescribable gift!

2 Corinthians 9:15

*F*EBRUARY 25, 2019

Yesterday after running errands we arrived home, and Emilio parked the car in the driveway. Eden had fallen asleep on the drive home, so I rolled down the windows and held her. A cool breeze came in through the window as I listened to the birds chirping and the leaves of the trees rustling in the wind. I could also hear the neighborhood kids laughing, and airplanes flying overhead, dogs barking, and a man and little girl walking by with their dog; the girl said words that I couldn't understand, but she sounded adorable. I hate to admit, really hate to admit, that those sounds used to annoy me, but I sat there soaking them in and delighting my whole heart in them. I felt almost like I was in California at the beach on a sunny day enjoying people enjoy other people.

I sat that way in the car for nearly two hours as the sun was peaking through the clouds and shining into the car on my face. It was a wonderful heavenly feeling. I could have sat there another hour just delighting in Eden and the sounds. I took my light grey scarf with flowers on it and draped it over Eden to keep her cozy and hide her eyes from the sun. Eventually, she woke up and looked at me with eyes half open and said, "Mama I hear children playing...." I said, "How wonderful! I hear them too. Did you know the Bible talks about heaven being like children playing in the streets?" Her eyes got big as I explained more.

I had forgotten exactly where the verse was in the Bible, but it was familiar because I had meditated on it deeply a couple of years ago. God kindly reminded me of its location that very night when my friend Karen messaged me the exact verse unaware that I had spoken of it to Eden earlier in the day. It's in Zechariah and reads:

"And the streets of the city shall be full of boys and girls playing in the streets thereof." (Zechariah.8:5)

One commentary says this verse is "denoting a large increase of inhabitants, in a literal sense; and may spiritually signify the large numbers of converts, of newborn babes, who are regenerated by the grace and Spirit of God, and are accounted of by the Lord for a generation: playing the streets thereof; being in health and rigour, and in great security."

What a glorious thought. No wonder I meditated on this verse years ago.

Later that day a sweet message arrived from my friend Alicia in California who has three children. One is graduating soon, which explains why she wrote what she did. It encouraged me, and maybe it will you as well:

"Oh, the wonderful heartbreak of motherhood! It is such an incredible blessing to watch your kids grow and learn and such a heartbreak knowing the world that waits trying to ensnare them! It is so difficult sometimes to share them and let others be a part of their influence! I never understood the pain that God went through in giving up Jesus to

the world as well as I did once I had children...
although I know that I don't even understand the
pain at the same level as God....oh I would never
claim that!!...but I understood that small bit more
once I had children and could never imagine giving them up for any kind of sacrifice! It makes me
so much more humbled before God for the sacrifice He made by sending Jesus for us! Motherhood
is the greatest heartbreaking blessing ever!! I will
pray for you as you are going through this with
Eden! She is a precious gift from God. The hardest
lesson I had to learn (and still struggle with) is that
these precious children that God gives us belong
to Him first! We are entrusted with their care here
on earth, but we cannot care for them more than
our Lord. Such hard lessons."

Thanks be to God for His indescribable gift!

2 Corinthians 9:15

❧ MUSIC ☙

Come, let us sing for joy to the Lord; let us shout aloud to the Rock of our salvation. Let us come before him with thanksgiving and extol him with music and song. For the Lord is the great God, the great King above all gods.

Psalm 95:1-3

*F*EBRUARY 27, 2019

Today Eden started singing, "God's been good to me. Oh, God's always been good." Then she added, "People are gettin' ready, Jesus is coming." It was beyond music to my ears. Perhaps that's how God feels when we sing to Him about Him. I write this to say we can never underestimate the power of music.

Case in point, I had a hard week and a half, and last night I went into Eden's room with her and put on Crystal Lewis (yes, from the late '90s). When her song, "Lord I Believe In You," came on I dissolved into tears in front of Eden. I don't think she has ever seen me cry like that. She stopped and stood frozen with big eyes. I just wept and worshipped and pointed to heaven. And she nodded like she understood and started dancing when "God's Been Good To Me" came on. I was still crying.

This little worship session lasted two hours. Eden was so well behaved the whole time. I let her in on my very private worship time, crying with the Lord and praising

Him. I told her, "These songs are for you too, Eden." With tears, I recounted to her how I had listened to these songs for hours and hours when I first became a Christian and that I would cry over them because of God's goodness.

When He saved me, I remember feeling like I was the only person on the planet that had that much love for Him, but the truth is He had an army of people that felt the same as I did, and He would later allow me to meet many of them.

During our worship time, I also pleaded with Eden, telling her that nothing else in the world matters but her coming to Christ. May God make it so.

Come, let us sing for joy to the Lord; let us shout aloud to the Rock of our salvation. Let us come before him with thanksgiving and extol him with music and song. For the Lord is the great God, the great King above all gods.

Psalm 95:1-3

⋺ GIVE ⋺

It is more blessed to give than to receive.

Acts 2:35

*M*ARCH 1, 2019

I decided to give away a dress that Eden had received as a gift, had never worn, and still had the tags on. She was starting to outgrow it, so I decided to bless a little girl in our church named Aletheia for her birthday.

The dress had this beautiful velvet material on the top and colorful silky type flower pattern on the bottom. To me, it looked like a perfect dress for Christmas. It wasn't any old dress either but was an Oscar de la Renta (did I even spell that correctly?). My Aunt Vicki, who is known for buying the best, had sent it to Eden. She is also known for clothing Eden from head to toe, and all the little girls at church too. We have hardly ever had to buy Eden anything, which is something we are *tremendously* grateful for.

I was preparing the gift with my friend Kristen and said to her, "This one is going to be hard to part with." And added, "but I'll give it away in faith and see what God does."

That was about two weeks ago.

Today a package arrived in the mail. I showed it to Eden as I rushed into her room with a hop in my step saying, "A gift! Let's open it and look inside."

My mom was sitting in the room too. Both she and Eden were like kids in a candy store waiting for the reveal...I opened the box and was so confused to see the Oscar de la Renta dress.

How did it get back to me? How did the dress I had just given away get in there? Then I stopped and realized that my Aunt Vicki had sent Eden the same dress only two sizes larger. I couldn't believe it.

And I screamed.

Then Eden screamed.

And so did my mom after I explained what had happened.

What a total blessing of what God can do when we give and trust and wait.

It is more blessed to give than to receive.

Acts 2:35

⌘ WORTHY ⌘

And I saw a strong angel proclaiming with a loud voice,
"Who is worthy to open the book and to break its seals?"

Revelation 5:2

*M*ARCH 2, 2019

A dear friend sent me a song tonight based on Revelation 5 by Chris Tomlin called "Is He Worthy?" She said the songs makes her teary. Eden and I loved it so much that we looked for, and listened to, every version of it on YouTube. Shane and Shane do an excellent version of it as well. I hope you'll give it a listen, and think of it as a catechism song for your children.

Just before bed, I had the song playing while I was sitting in my blue rocking chair. Eden was singing it word for word and said, "Mama, can you worship?" as to say she wanted to see me cry out to God and really praise Him. I told her I was worshipping, just quietly. How special. Then she started singing the song over and over, which was even more special.

Final note: We had our nightly devotion by the fireplace and Eden didn't want to stop praying. She kept saying, "Mama pray for so and so, and so and so, and so and so." I'm most thankful for Eden's desire to pray tonight because without it I know I would not have prayed for half our church like we did.

Eden and I praying for a dear brother in our church
after one of our ladies' Bible studies.

And I saw a strong angel proclaiming with a loud voice,
"Who is worthy to open the book and to break its seals?

Revelation 5:2

❧ HELP ☙

God is our refuge and strength, A very present help in trouble.

Psalm 46:1

*M*ARCH 3, 2019

Today Eden and Aletheia wore their dresses to church. What a special day! This is one dress I may have to hold onto because it serves as a great reminder of God's grace and hand of kindness; like an Ebenezer rock.

This article from GotQuestions.org explains just what I mean:

> Most of us are familiar with the name "Ebenezer" because of the character Ebenezer Scrooge in Charles Dickens's novella *A Christmas Carol*. Because of that story, the name "Ebenezer" has taken on the connotation of miserliness and a lack of charity—although, to be fair, Ebenezer Scrooge did become a changed man at the end of the story.
>
> The name "Ebenezer" actually comes from the Bible. In 1 Samuel 7, during the end of the time of the judges, Israel experiences revival under the leadership of Samuel. The nation repents of their sin, destroys their idols, and begins to seek the Lord. Samuel gathered the people at Mizpah where they confessed their sin, and Samuel offered a sacrifice on their behalf.

It was during this time of repentance and renewal that the enemy attacked: "While Samuel was sacrificing the burnt offering, the Philistines drew near to engage Israel in battle" (v.10). The Israelites went out to do battle against the invaders, and God sent them supernatural help: "That day the LORD thundered with loud thunder against the Philistines and threw them into such a panic that they were routed before the Israelites."

Israel's victory over the Philistines was decisive. Several cities the Philistines had captured were restored to Israel, and it was a long time before the Philistines tried to invade Israel again. To commemorate the divine victory, "Samuel took a stone and set it up between Mizpah and Shen. He named it Ebenezer, saying, 'Thus far the LORD has helped us'" (verse 12).

Ebenezer means "stone of help." From then on, every time an Israelite saw the stone erected by Samuel, he would have a tangible reminder of the Lord's power and protection. The "stone of help" marked the spot where the enemy had been routed and God's promise to bless His repentant people had been honored. The Lord had helped them, all the way to Ebenezer.

God is our refuge and strength, A very present help in trouble.

Psalm 46:1

❧ REJOICE ☙

There is neither Jew nor Greek, there is neither slave nor free man, there is neither male nor female; for you are all one in Christ Jesus.

Galatians 3:28

*M*ARCH 4, 2019

Excerpt from *The Faith Shaped Life* by Ian Hamilton that ministered to me today:

The Christian life is a life of constant, unhindered joy—or at least, so says the Apostle Paul: 'Rejoice in the Lord always; again I will say, Rejoice' (Phil. 4:4). According to Paul, joy is not to be an occasional feature in the believer's life; it is to be a constant reality, a daily, moment-by-moment reality. Does this seem a somewhat unreal expectation? Is Paul expecting too much? Is he even living in the real world, where disappointments, discouragements, and disasters can, and do, blast the believer's life? Is it not the height of spiritual escapism to think that Christians should always be rejoicing?

We can hardly, however, accuse Paul of engaging in spiritual escapism, or of suggesting that believers live trouble-free lives. For one thing, his own life was a catalogue of disappointments, discouragements, and disasters (read 2 Cor. 11:23-29); and for another, he never tired of telling Christians that

the life of faith was a life beset with trials, temptations, and persecutions (read Acts 14:21, 22;2 Tim
3:10-12). Paul was no head-in-the-cloud Christian. He well knew, by bitter experience, the pains
and sorrows of the believing life. And yet, he still
writes, 'Rejoice in the Lord always'; and in case we
don't quite take in the force of what he has said, he
repeats himself, 'again I will say, Rejoice.'

Paul is well aware of how seemingly impossible his
command (for that is what it is) will appear to us.
But in no sense is Paul suggesting that Christians
will always have the sunshine of God's love and
goodness shining on their backs, making it easy for
them to rejoice. What he is saying, however, is that
in spite of all the troubles and discouragements
and disasters that can, and do, overtake the child
of God, he is still able to 'rejoice.' How can that be?

Look carefully at what Paul writes: 'Rejoice in the
Lord.' The Christian is to rejoice always because
his joy is pre-eminently located not in his circumstances, but in his Saviour--in the unchanging and
unchangeable Lord Jesus Christ! Paul is not saying
for one moment that believers should be walking
around with a permanent grin, saying 'Praise the
Lord!' every second sentence. For one thing, this
is not the picture Scriptures give us of our Lord
Jesus, the proto-typical man of faith. Our Saviour
knew the sore reality of disappointments and discouragements; he experienced the greatest weariness; he was 'despised and rejected by men.' Christians are able to 'Rejoice always' because our joy is
in who our God and Saviour is and in what he has
done for us, and nothing can change his love for us,
or change the constancy of his faithful character.
This means that no matter what befalls a Christian, he is still a child of God, a forgiven sinner, a

heaven-bound saint, the most blessed being in the cosmos! If the Christian loses everything, he still has everything, for he cannot lose his Saviour, who is his great salvation (2 Cor 6:10).

Martin Luther saw this and concluded his great Reformation hymn, 'A Mighty Fortress is Our God,' with these words:

> *Let goods and kindred go,*
> *this mortal life also;*
> *The body they may kill:*
> *God's truth abideth still;*
> *His kingdom is forever.*

Paul is not saying that the Christian will always appear to be full of joy; but even through the bitterest of tears, the believing heart can rejoice in the Lord. Even in times of deepest and darkest perplexity, the Child of God can rejoice, not because he can fully understand God's ways with him, but because he has a Saviour, who loved him and gave himself for him, and who loves him now and forever.

Christian joy can at times be 'out of this world' (1 Pet. 1:8). At other times it may be covered by an avalanche of trials and discouragements. But can we not always rejoice, seeing that our Lord Jesus is God over all, blessed forever; that he, who bore our sin and shame, is seated on the throne of the universe; that one day we shall see him as he is, and be forever with him? Jesus is our cause for constant rejoicing."

(*The Faith Shaped Life*, Ian Hamilton, Pages 46-48)

There is neither Jew nor Greek, there is neither slave nor free man, there is neither male nor female; for you are all one in Christ Jesus.

Galatians 3:28

❧ REWARDS ❧

Behold, children are a gift of the LORD, The fruit of the womb is a reward.

Psalm 127:3

*M*ARCH 5, 2019

When I see a comment on Facebook encouraging a mother to "enjoy every second" with her children my heart always aches a bit. I think to myself, "In what ways can I possibly enjoy Eden more?" I already let my house-cleaning lapse so I can "enjoy every second." Emilio rarely complains. I also seek God often on ways to enjoy Eden while redeeming the time, and the one thing I love to do is teach her the Word of God through worship songs.

Like the day I made up a tune for Psalm 23 and recorded it on my phone. Eden asks me to play it over and over in the car. One day as I was changing her diaper she began quoting all of Psalm 23. What a joy to be able to teach her Scripture that will stick (hopefully) in this life, right into heaven.

Tonight I decided to ask her questions about heaven. It was an easy transition since we were reading a Winnie the Pooh story where Pooh is having "honey trouble." He can't find honey to fill his rumbly tummy, so he dreams about a land over-flowing with honey. I told Eden about The Promise Land and that heaven will be like a land flowing with milk and honey. I told her that the bees in heaven won't sting and we will never eat too much honey.

I asked, "Will we be able to sin there?" She answered, "No."

"Will there be tears?" No, again.

I explained that there is a verse that says the Lord will wipe every tear away, so any tears will be wonderful tears, for all God has done. "Just like when Mama worships and cries, it's not sad tears but tears of deep appreciation and love."

"Will the lions bite there?" "*No*," she answered.

"Will the cats scratch there?" "*No.*"

"Will dogs bite?" "*No.*"

We had much fun going back and forth before bed, and hearing her answers was a delight.

Speaking of going to bed...Eden has started resisting going to sleep, but thankfully I've noticed that a few steps we've implemented are helping. If she is about to get upset about going to bed, I tell her, "The Bible says not to go to bed in your anger." And I can't tell you how many nights God used that verse to snap her right out of a full-blown cry fest. Then I tell her, "God can help you, and I understand where you are coming from. I want to stay up with you too, but you need sleep and so do I. God is the only one who never has to sleep. Isn't that amazing? In fact, He tells us that he will give His beloved sleep."

I've also found giving her a short transition time is a big help. I'll tell her, "Why don't you put your baby Happy away and make her cozy for tomorrow and put your things in special spots and when you wake up, they will be there." Tonight she did just that.

She has a little mini Barbie with long hair that one of the sweet ladies (JoAnn) from church gave her. Eden has washed her hair countless times and given her just as many baths, and tonight, she tucked her in with a diaper wipe (so funny and adorable). She asked me, "Mama, may I have a wipe?" How could I turn her down? She made the blanket with the wipe and put a prayer book by her and said "she can read this in the morning," then kissed her and hugged her. I then picked Eden up to take her to bed, and she did not resist sleep at all. Maybe doing transitions like this will help your children too.

I have started to do this with our family devotion time as well. I'll prepare Eden with what I expect from her, which helps her to adjust better than if I just grab her and say this is what we are doing. It seems to get her mind ready for what is about to happen, and she feels included in the plan. Which is biblical if you ask me because God has included us in *His* plan.

I'll leave you with a laugh:

Eden loves to "do my hair."

Tonight, I asked her who taught her to do hair the way she does.

She said, "Mephibosheth."

Ha! Eden Joy for sure lives up to her middle name.

Behold, children are a gift of the LORD, The fruit of the womb is a reward.

Psalm 127:3

❧ LIGHT ❧

What then shall we say to these things? If God is for us, who is against us?

Romans 8:31

*M*ARCH 6, 2019

A few answers to prayer I'm grateful for today:

1. I prayed Eden would want to do my hair, and she did several times today. It was the most adorable thing. She would say, "Lay back, Mama."

2. I prayed Eden would have more affection for her baby dolls than for her stuffed animals. Not that she can't love those too, but I'm sure you know what I mean. It seems so natural for children to have a love for animals, but maybe not as much for other children. After all, most children's books are of animals talking, singing, praying, hopping and dancing. I saw in Eden more of a pull to animals than babies, much like I had growing up, and I want her to be different, by God's grace. And lately, after much prayer, she has been playing a lot with two babies she calls Baby Happy and Baby Noe (short for Noelle). Often when I pray, I will pray in front of her for her.

3. Eden has been very kind lately (a lot of sleep helps and good food), and she has been telling me she

loves me a lot, which is music to my ringing ears. If you know me, you know I battle ringing in the ears. I can have high-pitched ringing for two weeks at a time, non-stop. Eden has been a wonderful distraction from my physical maladies.

Praise God for His answered prayers and for His Word that is living and active and able to guide, and is a lamp to my feet and light to my path. Here are a few verses that helped sustain me in the waiting:

> *"The statutes of the LORD are right, rejoicing the heart: the commandment of the LORD is pure, enlightening the eyes."* Psalm 19:8

> *"O send out thy light and thy truth: let them lead me; let them bring me unto thy holy hill, and to thy tabernacles."* Psalm 43:3

> *"For the commandment is a lamp; and the law is light; and reproofs of instruction are the way of life:"* Proverbs 6:23

> *"For thou wilt light my candle: the LORD my God will enlighten my darkness."* Psalm 18:28

If any of you reading this are in a weary place, take heart that God can and is able to light your candle. Notice in Psalm 18:28 (above) that there are no lit candles until *the Lord lights them.*

We cannot muster up a flame. He has to do it. Which then makes me think of abiding. We must abide in Him if we are to bear good fruit of any kind, like Jesus talked about in John 15:4, "Abide in Me, and I in you. As the branch cannot bear fruit of itself unless it abides in the vine, so neither can you unless you abide in Me."

The word abide is the Greek word μεινατε (meinate) which means to remain, abide, stay, wait. I learned Greek with Emilio many moons ago, and it finally paid off in this book. There. I used Greek!

May we all remain and wait, and abide and wait, and stay and wait on the Lord to move on our behalf.

What then shall we say to these things? If God is for us, who is against us?

Romans 8:31

⋟ LAUGHTER ⋞

But for you who fear My name, the sun of righteousness will rise with healing in its wings;

Malachi 4:2

MARCH 7, 2019

Today was a good day. Eden was being sweet. We sat outside blowing bubbles and walked on the wall in our backyard. I also picked her up really high and let her sit on my head as we walked around. Playing with her is better than a gym workout. My mom thinks I'm getting too thin and I tell her having a toddler will do that to you, not to mention that my diet is free of dairy, gluten, egg, and oats, all of which I'm avoiding to heal my thyroid, if God should choose.

I take medicine for my thyroid (Hashimoto's Thyroiditis) and have been able to go from 75mg of medication a day to 50mg. At one point, around 15 years ago, I was at 88mg, so perhaps my body is healing slowly. I'm thinking about writing a book on how God helped me in the healing process. I don't take for granted the days that I feel well. Bad days bring ringing in the ears and fatigue, which I try to push through. Some days I wonder how I'll keep living like this. I'm glad I have Eden to help take my mind off it all.

Like today, while in Eden's room, I put on a worship song that says,

"Love, love, love one another and be kind.

Jesus taught us to love Him so let your light shine."

It has a fun beat, and Eden started running around the room, so I put a little agility course together where she could run in a circle and hop over things. I started running, and demonstrating what to do and she started laughing terribly hard. When she tried to run and hop herself, it was so cute. Her hop was more like a skip. It was just adorable, and if I think about it too long, I will cry. It reminded me of heaven, actually, where perhaps the simplest things will be a deep joy for us.

Proverbs 10:6 says, "Blessings are on the head of the righteous." Lord, please allow me to see more days like this. And allow my sisters reading this the same. May we all experience sweet days of blessings on our heads. Amen.

Tonight I asked Eden, "How does someone become a Christian?" She said as clear as day, "By God saving them." Amen. I wonder how much of that she understands. Only God knows.

Before bed, she wanted to play with my hair and said, "Lay back." So I did what I thought she wanted, which was to recline myself a little bit, but she said "No! Like this!" and she got on the carpet and laid flat on the floor. I laughed hard. I have no idea where she learned that. Then she got a face-wipe and wiped my whole face and said, "You are all done."

Right before bed, I listened to "Is He Worthy?" by Chris Tomlin. I let Eden join in and see me cry a bit. She seems to have really taken a liking to the song. Thank you, Kristen Rasor, for sending it to me. And thank you, Lord, for good days like today. Not perfect days, but pain-free ones. Days where we can breathe easy and pretend that there is no evil in the world, even if just for one day. Thank you most of all that there is coming a day when that will be a reality.

But for you who fear My name, the sun of righteousness will rise with healing in its wings;

Malachi 4:2

❧ FAITH ☙

Therefore, since we are surrounded by so great a cloud of witnesses, let us also lay aside every weight, and sin which clings so closely, and let us run with endurance the race that is set before us, looking to Jesus, the founder and perfecter of our faith, who for the joy that was set before him endured the cross, despising the shame, and is seated at the right hand of the throne of God. Consider him who endured from sinners such hostility against himself, so that you may not grow weary or fainthearted.

Hebrews 12:1–3

---

*M*ARCH 8, 2019

Tonight I read an article from Melissa B. Kruger, the author of *5 Things To Pray For Your Kids*. Be encouraged:

"From the moment I held my newborn baby in my arms for the first time, I understood my complete dependence on the Lord in new ways. Becoming a mother awakened me to my own inadequacy— there was so much I couldn't control, so much I couldn't do, but this little baby depended on me to take care of her. So, I prayed and asked God for help. It became a moment-by-moment conversation, and I gained a new understanding of what it was to pray without ceasing:

Lord, please help her be able to nurse.

Lord, help me understand why she's crying.

Lord, please help her to fall asleep.

Lord, help her fever to go down.

Lord, give me wisdom.

Lord, help me.

As my children have grown, I've continued to pray for the daily circumstances of their lives: friendships, sports, health, test scores. And, these are good things to pray for our children—the Lord invites us to cast all our cares on him. However, as I've read and studied Paul's prayers for those he loved, I've also realized the fundamental importance of praying for my children's spiritual needs. Some days, in the busyness of living, these are forgotten. Yet, my children's greatest need is not temporary happiness, but increasing holiness. Holiness and happiness are not in opposition to one another, but are integrally linked. Holiness leads to true happiness: the eternal joy of a soul rooted in Christ. I'm praying for my child's best and highest good when I ask God to make them holy. Paul's prayer for the Philippians has helped guide my prayers for their holiness in four ways. 'And it is my prayer that your love may abound more and more, with knowledge and all discernment, so that you may approve what is excellent, and so be pure and blameless for the day of Christ, filled with the fruit of righteousness that comes through Jesus Christ, to the glory and praise of God' (Phil. 1:9-11).

Affection

We rightly desire good behavior in our children. (Please stop throwing your Cheerios on the floor and hitting your sister!) However, our ultimate goal is more than outward obedience, we want inward affection for God. Just like Paul, we can pray our children's love for the Lord would abound more and more with each passing year. Only God can give them new hearts that beat with deep affection and delight for Jesus. May our children love the Lord with all their heart.

Knowledge

Every day our children are learning. They learn to tie their shoes, to count to ten, to put their plate in the dishwasher, and one day, they'll learn to drive a car (this will provide a new opportunity to pray without ceasing). They're also learning about God. Pray that the Bible stories they learn, the Scripture they memorize, and the sermons they hear would lay a strong foundation of knowledge that would provide a spiritual lens through which they understand the world. May our children love the Lord with all their mind.

Discernment

Today your child may be struggling to decide which lunch box to choose, but one day they'll be making choices that shape the course of their lives. They'll need discernment to know what friends to choose, which job to pursue, and who to marry. Their ability to make wise choices begins with a right reverence of the Lord. Pray that your child will be able to discern what is good and seek the Lord for wisdom. May our children love the Lord with all their soul.

Fruit

We often think of success in terms of money, fame, or academic excellence. However, God's goal for our children is something more, something better, something eternal: a harvest of righteousness. It's not something they can attain on their own (or something we can force). It's the fruit of a heart that seeks the Lord. We often attempt to produce righteousness outside of relationship, but it's only by the Spirit's power that our children can bloom into people of love, joy, peace, patience, kindness, goodness, faithfulness, gentleness, and self-control. So, we pray, asking the Gardener of their soul to produce a plentiful harvest. May our children love the Lord with all their strength.

We have so many hopes for our children. We want them to be healthy and happy and for circumstances to go well. However, more than perfect health or circumstances, our children need the Lord. Teach them His Word, teach them to pray, and, most of all, ask the Lord to be at work in their hearts, doing immeasurably more than we can even imagine.

May our children love the Lord with all their heart.

May our children love the Lord with all their mind.

May our children love the Lord with all their soul.

May our children love the Lord with all their strength."

I take those words to heart from Melissa Kruger, and as I lay in bed, my thoughts turn to the day Eden will drive a car, which makes my stomach drop, and my heart ache. I don't know how I'll handle it. I guess the answer is, by faith.

Just like we go to sleep by faith.

We eat by faith.

We drive by faith.

We fly by faith.

We work by faith.

We get married by faith.

We have children by faith.

We buy homes by faith.

We are saved by faith.

We plant ourselves in churches by faith.

We die by faith.

By faith, according to Strong's Greek, speaks of belief, trust, confidence; fidelity, faithfulness. And faith has accomplished much through history. Case in point:

> "...who through faith subdued kingdoms, wrought righteousness, obtained promises, stopped the mouths of lions." Hebrews 11:33

> "By faith Abel offered unto God a more excellent sacrifice than Cain, by which he obtained witness that he was righteous, God testifying of his gifts: and by it he being dead yet speaketh..." Hebrews 11:4-8,17

> "...so that you will not be sluggish, but imitators of those who through faith and patience inherit the promises." Hebrews 6:12-15

> "My righteous one shall live by faith, and if he shrinks back, my soul has no pleasure in him." Hebrews 10:38

> "Look at the proud one; His soul is not upright--But the righteous will live by his faith." Habakkuk 2:4

> "For the gospel reveals the righteousness of God that comes by faith from start to finish, just as it is written: 'The righteous will live by faith.'" Romans 1:17

> "And it is clear that no one is justified before God by the Law, because, 'The righteous will live by faith.'" Galatians 3:11

I have to admit I need to read my own book many times over until these truths change me.

By the way, the Greek word πιστεως (pisteōs), which means "faith" is pronounced (from what I've learned) "peace toes", which makes me think that when our feet walk by faith, God blesses our *toes* off with *peace*.

If you have made it this far in my book, God bless you. I covet your prayers for my whole family.

And may God strengthen each of you as you read. May you sense that you are being washed and renewed and that your time was well spent. I thank you for your precious time. May we have all eternity to talk about all the ways the Lord has sustained you and helped you in this race.

Therefore, since we are surrounded by so great a cloud of witnesses, let us also lay aside every weight, and sin which clings so closely, and let us run with endurance the race that is set before us, looking to Jesus, the founder and perfecter of our faith, who for the joy that was set before him endured the cross, despising the shame, and is seated at the right hand of the throne of God. Consider him who endured from sinners such hostility against himself, so that you may not grow weary or fainthearted.

Hebrews 12:1–3

❧ WITNESS ☙

Faithful are the wounds of a friend,

Proverbs 27:6

*M*ARCH 9, 2019

Eden heard a siren when we were outside walking. She said, "Hmmm, this makes me sad." I don't recall ever saying those words to her after hearing a siren. Typically, I tell her that we should say a prayer in case someone is hurt.

A little later she asked me again, "Is Mama a Christian?" I said, "Yes."

"Is Eden a Christian?" she asked as her eyes squinted.

I said, "Let me ask you...is Eden a Christian?"

She said, "No, not yet."

"When will you be a Christian?" I asked.

She said, "One day."

So I told her the gospel in pieces. Sometimes I think she truly understands, other times I am not sure, so I just keep talking to her like she can understand because one day she will.

After our walk, I received a lovely message from a sister, Marie, in our church. I posted today on Facebook about how my shopping experience was miserable because I had forgotten my tracts at home.

She said, "Was watching your video on how you forgot your tracts. Am always so encouraged by the example you set by sharing the Gospel everywhere you go. I know it's all of God's grace to you. It spurs me on. Remembered this Scripture that I loved and saved in my notes to memorize. May God continue to bless your efforts for His glory. 'Those who have insight will shine brightly like the brightness of the expanse of heaven, and those who lead the many to righteousness, like the stars forever and ever.' Daniel 12:3"

I thought it might encourage you reading this to not waste your trips to the grocery store or the bank or the gas station or Costco or the pet store or the mall or wherever life finds you. I love passing out tracts that have a message about the Lord.

A Christian friend recently told me that he "doesn't like gospel tracts." So I thought I'd give a few reasons as to why I use gospel tracts (oh and I don't pass out just any tract - it must have a solid, and clear gospel message on it). And, yes, you can still be a Christian even if you don't pass out tracts. As long as you're being a witness and testifying of Christ, then that is wonderful (and this obviously can be done without the use of tracts). The critical question for a Christian is, "Am I obeying the great commission?" Are you telling others about the Lord? Are you opening your mouth to preach the Good News of what Jesus Christ has done?

If you're like me, you want to preach the Good News with everyone you meet. When private talk and conversation is not convenient, tracts are a handy tool to keep in your handbag or back pocket to help you be an effective witness to reach the lost.

Here's why I think tracts are effective ways to reach people (in no particular order):

1. People can get saved by reading one—it has happened before and can happen again.

2. Tracts go where you can't (like into someone's house or in a handbag, pocket, etc. to be read later).

3. Tracts don't lose their cool - they stick right to the gospel message - they don't get into arguments.

4. Folks can read it over and over (I was standing in the check out line at a store and turned around to hand the lady behind me a Million Dollar Bill gospel tract. She immediately reached in her purse and pulled out an old worn out Million Dollar Bill tract. "I think you need a new one," I said. She laughed and took it." Make sure you read the back...it has a gospel message on it," I added.

5. If there are verses on them, we have God's promise that His Word will not come back void.

6. They are a great door opener for the gospel to be preached.

7. They make you more giving - I use my own money to purchase tracts.

8. They can do the witnessing for us. I try to speak to everyone that I give a tract to, but if you are timid and afraid to open your mouth just hand out a tract (I must very timid because my purse has about 500 tracts in it right now).

9. Good tracts that have a clear gospel presentation bring glory to God—whether anyone ever gets saved from them.

10. They are a natural way of communication.

11. They help keep us prepared and alert to share the gospel with anyone we meet.

12. They remind us that God is Sovereign. Every encounter we have throughout our day is a Divine

encounter. That awareness, coupled with good tracts, helps us to be good stewards of the breath and life God has given us.

13. They help us find other believers. It's neat to hand someone a tract and find out that he or she is brother or sister in Christ. I can't tell you how many times I've been encouraged to keep pressing on after talking to a fellow believer that received a tract. My friend Mike O. met a lady in a donut shop one morning, and she was so thrilled another Christian was concerned about sharing the Gospel.

14. Didn't God give us one big tract, the Holy Bible?

15. Tracts are a great way to keep your children focused on souls when they are out and about, instead of looking at the outside of people.

I'm sure there are many other reasons.

"When preaching and private talk are not available, you need to have a tract ready. Get good striking tracts, or none at all. But a touching gospel tract may be the seed of eternal life. Therefore, do not go out without your tracts." Charles Spurgeon

Ray Comfort wrote this on the subject:

"There is an old story of how a diver saw a piece of paper clutched in the mouth of an oyster. The man grabbed it, found that it was a gospel tract and said, 'I can't hold out any longer. His mercy is so great that He has caused His Word to follow me even to the bottom of the ocean.' God used a tract to save the man. Why should a Christian use tracts? Simply, because God uses them. He used a tract to save the great missionary Hudson Taylor, as well as many, many others. That fact alone should be enough incentive for a Christian to always use tracts to reach the lost, but there are even more reasons why we should use them. Here are a few:

- Tracts can make an opening for us to share our faith. We can watch people's reaction as we give them a tract, and see if they are open to listening to spiritual things.

- They can do the witnessing for us. If we are too timid to speak to someone about the things of God, we can at least give them a tract, or leave it lying around so that someone will pick it up.

- They speak to the person when they are ready—i.e. they don't read it until they want to.

- They can find their way into people's homes when we can't.

- They don't get into argument. They just state their case.

Dr. Oswald J. Smith said, 'The only way to carry out the Great Commission will be by the means of the printed page.' Billy Graham said, 'Nothing surpasses a tract for sowing the seed of the Good News.' The Apostle Paul said, 'I might by any means save some.' I'm sure that if Paul had access to the printed page that we have access to, he would carry his convictions to the full.

I am never in public without gospel tracts. In fact, if anyone ever finds me in public without them, I will give them $1,000. That makes sure I am always loaded for battle (you should say the same thing to your friends). When I see an attendant who is standing in a store looking bored, I can give him or her a tract and say, 'This will break your boredom.' Most people smile, and say 'Thanks.' In fact, we have tracts especially to break boredom. One is called the Intelligence Test Bookmark (available from Living Waters Publications). This tract has a ten-minute 'getaway' time. After you give it to them, you have ten minutes to get away, before they even know that it's a Christian tract. Other titles are specially designed for specific purposes.

If you want people to accept your tract from you, don't say, 'Would you like this?' They will probably say, 'What is it?' and then you're in trouble. Instead, say, 'Did you get one of these?' That question has a two-fold effect. You stir up curiosity and make them ask 'One of what?' That's when you pass it to them. That phrase also makes them feel as though they are missing out on something. And so they are.

Perhaps your whole life seems to pass before your eyes at the thought of giving someone a tract. Don't worry – you are not alone. We all battle fear. The answer to fear is found in the prayer closet. Ask God to give you compassion that will swallow your fears. Meditate on the fate of the ungodly. Give Hell some deep thought. Confront what it is that you are so fearful of.

Do you like roller coasters? Some Christians want to try bungee jumping or sky diving. Isn't it strange? We are prepared to risk our lives for the love of fear... and yet we are willing to let a sinner go to Hell for the fear of giving out a tract. Ask yourself how many piles of bloodied stones you can find where Christians have been stoned to death for preaching the gospel. How much singed soil can you find where they have been burned at the stake. Shame on us. We have a fear of rejection. We are fearful of looking foolish. That's a subtle form of pride. That sort of fear isn't from God. He hasn't given us the spirit of fear. If we listen to the lies of the devil rather than the Word of God, it shows we prefer to have faith in the devil rather than in our faithful Creator. What a terrible thought! Faith in His "precious promises" will lift us above the fear that so easily paralyzes us. If God is with us, nothing can be against us.

If you have never given out tracts, leave them in a shopping cart, or put them in the mail when you pay bills. Why not begin today? Then each night as you shut your eyes to go to sleep, you will have something very special to pray about... that God will use the tract you put somewhere. You will also have a deep sense of satisfaction, that you played a small part in carrying out the Great Commission... to reach this dying world with the gospel of everlasting life. Don't waste your life. Do something for the Kingdom of God while you are able to. Finally, always remember – treat every day as though it were your last... one day you will be right, so do something for God while you are able."

Faithful are the wounds of a friend,

Proverbs 27:6

ꙅ FEARS ꙴ

*M*ARCH 10, 2019

Tonight Eden asked again before bed if she was a Christian.

She said, "No. Not yet" when I asked her to answer the question.

I talked to her about the gospel briefly. I asked her, "Where does God live?"

"Heaven," she replied.

I asked her if you could "see heaven?"

She said, "No."

I asked, "Where is heaven?"

She pointed up with her most adorable hand (that I wish would stay small forever).

I said, "I want to teach you something new so pay close attention.

Where does Satan 'the serpent' live?"

She said, "Heaven."

"Nooooooo," I said as I shook my head.

"Let me ask you again...where does Satan 'the serpent' live?"

She said, "In the tree?"

Wow. She is truly listening. She was thinking of the tree from the Garden of Eden.

Incredible.

So I explained that he lives in the pit and pointed down. And a pit it is!

What an enemy of God he is.

May Jesus come quickly to this dark earth and shine His great light.

Speaking of earth, we had a terrible storm last night that sounded like it could produce a tornado. It reminded me that this earth is not our home, and what a terrible thing the fall was in the Garden.

The storm woke all of us up at 5:00am. Eden wouldn't go back to sleep for another two hours. At one point, she sat in our bed staring at the lightning flickering in the windows. "It's raining," she would say. And boy if only she knew all that was happening outside. I knew though, and have to admit my nerves were on edge...bad. Truth is, I don't trust the Lord the way I ought to (this is a confession book, right?)

I have never liked lightning storms, and the ones in Texas are no joke.

When we moved to Texas in January of 2007, we had a storm break out like clockwork, for what felt like months, at about 3:00 every afternoon. The first time it happened, I literally ran into a closet in the middle of our home and cried out to God. I decided to keep a Bible and blanket and flashlight in there for the next day. It began happening so frequently that I left it all in there for good.

After a decade of living here, I thought I was getting over my fear of storms, (remember I'm from California), but I guess my love and trust for the Lord is not strong enough, and He still wants to teach me some things. Please pray for me in that.

May the Lord help us to overcome our fears. Let's confess to Him tonight anything that troubles us. He already knows about it but He delights to hear the prayers of His children. You love to have your children come to you when they are troubled or happy or whatever the mood or situation is and I imagine the Lord is the same (Matt 11:28).

There is no fear in love; but perfect love casts out fear, because fear involves punishment, and the one who fears is not perfected in love.

1 John 4:18

❧ PRICELESS ☙

So if you who are evil know how to give good gifts to your children, how much more will your Father in heaven give good things to those who ask Him!

Matthew 7:11

$\mathcal{M}$ARCH 12, 2019

Today Eden said, "Mama, I don't love the serpent. I love God."

I thought, "How special" because I don't ever remember piecing those words together like that or teaching her to say that. May it be true.

She then told me she "wants to be on David's team, not Goliath's team."

Oh, how I pray that for her every day.

Later that evening, I was in the kitchen tidying things up when Eden came in and handed me two diaper wipes with some things wrapped inside and said, "Here Mama... here's a gift for you." I had noticed her earlier being up to something in the living room. I kindly thanked her with much affection, but was in a hurry to get her in bed and never unwrapped the gift.

After she was sound asleep, I walked back into the dimly lit kitchen to find my gift. She watches me wrap gifts for different people and children often, what could hers possible be for me?

It was crayons. Eden had wrapped the only "gift" she could think to give in her diaper wipe "wrapping paper."

The way I felt was indescribable. May God give Eden the ultimate gift of salvation in Christ. The One who was wrapped in a swaddling cloth that more than likely cost less than my entire pack of diaper wipes, and was laid in a manger next to lowly animals, but Who was (and is) of infinite worth. "Thanks be to God for His indescribable gift!" (2 Corinthians 9:15)

So if you who are evil know how to give good gifts to your children, how much more will your Father in heaven give good things to those who ask Him!

Matthew 7:11

❧ WORRY ☙

*M*ARCH 13, 2019

Today Eden and I were in our spare bedroom cleaning out some things when we found beautiful twin baby dolls I had bought for her a few months back. I thought they were so pretty, that I just had to buy them. One has green eyes and the other blue. She said, "Look! The twins! Can we feed them, Mama?" I said, "Of course."

Before we gave them "food" I prayed that she would have twins one day, and that she would marry a humble man. Twins run in my family, so it's very possible.

I have to admit that I often think about the day we will give Eden away in marriage. And it's dreadful. I have sobbed hard over it many nights. So, instead of being consumed with that I want to commit it to prayer...

Lord, thank you first for the opportunity to pray for this. That I'm not powerless in the sense that your Word says that the "effectual fervent prayer of the righteous accomplishes much." And I have seen You accomplish much in the past. I have seen your faithfulness. Instead of "giving her away," help it be more of "gaining a son", and a ton of godly offspring. That our home will literally become full because of Eden. Please end a cycle of barrenness that was on both sides of my family (my dad had three sisters [one set of twins], and none had children. My mom had one brother, and he did not have kids either) and help Eden not to be like me where I didn't have a child till almost 40. If it is Your will, when Eden gets married, allow our wounds of missing her to heal right away with a grandchild or twins. And if it pleases you, may Eden and I look back on this prayer and laugh with joy because of how You fulfilled it. I also pray for the ladies reading this that you would mend any wounded hearts with special surprises from heaven. In Christ's name. Amen.

Perhaps you can take a minute and do the same thing. Instead of allowing your worry or care to overtake you let's take it to God in prayer.

Take My yoke upon you and learn from Me, for I am gentle and humble in heart, and you will find rest for your souls.

Matthew 11:29

❧ REDEEM ❧

I trust in You, O LORD; I say, "You are my God." My times are in Your hands;

Psalm 31:14-15a

*M*ARCH 14, 2019 am

Eden told me this morning, "Mama, you are a gift from God." She said it before bed too, at one point grabbing my face and kissing my cheek. How do I get over this? Lord, thank you for these gifts I don't deserve, I gladly accept them.

It's painful how much Eden has grown. When I hold her, I can feel her legs dangling almost to my knees. It's as if they grew inches overnight. Shoes that were too big last week are now too small.

Lord, please help me redeem the time and not have regrets. I know perfection is not possible because we are in our fallen bodies, but help me daily to have joy and kindness and be creative and to be as close to blameless as possible. Amen.

Lord I pray for my dear readers that whatever season they find themselves in that they will serve the person in front of them with care and compassion and unto You.

Help them to redeem the time and press on to do as Elizabeth Elliot would say, "the next thing."

I trust in You, O LORD; I say, "You are my God." My times are in Your hands;

Psalm 31:14-15a

❧ PURPOSE ❧

And we know that God causes all things to work together for good to those who love God, to those who are called according to His purpose.

Romans 8:28

*M*ARCH 14, 2019 pm

Eden has been battling weird constipation that kept her up throughout the night. At one point, I just resolved we would have a slumber party. I sat on the carpet with her, and she began wanting to do my hair and then she (many times over) wanted to pray for her tummy and mine, that we could both have babies. I laughed. She got on her knees and said, "God you are able to do it." It was very special, and I prayed again for twins for her. Then she wanted to do my hair some more, which reminded me of a little girl named Ethni who long ago loved to do my hair. At the time, I couldn't get over how cute her arms were when she would pretend to blow it dry.

I told Eden all about Ethni. She wanted to hear more, so I told her about Kolaiah, Ethni's sister. About nine years ago, Kolaiah spent the night at our home, and as I tucked her into bed, she wanted me to pray for her and read to her out of Isaiah. Her request surprised me, as she was a very young child. I read to her, but was so choked up by her request and could hardly continue. She started to doze off and said, "I love you, Trisha."

I left her and went to my closet and cried for a good hour. I felt a deep love for her, and I told God that I couldn't ever handle the love of my own child. And I was right. God is going to have to help me as the love for Eden hurts. I know my mom feels the same for me. I told Eden all this, and she enjoyed listening to it. Then we prayed that we could see those two girls one day as they now live far away.

It turned out to be a special time. God can use even constipation for our good and His glory. Oh, and Eden said, "If God gives you a baby, Mama, I can pray for it." The sweetness and genuineness and child-likeness remind me of what heaven will be like.

And we know that God causes all things to work together for good to those who love God, to those who are called according to His purpose.

Romans 8:28

❧ LOVE ☙

May the Lord direct your hearts into the love of God and into the steadfastness of Christ.

2 Thessalonians 3:5

*M*ARCH 15, 2019

Before bed tonight I sang Eden a song from Psalm 119. It's a tune I made up in order to memorize the whole psalm, and she just loves it. And I love that she loves it. I bet God is that way. He loves when we love things He has come up with (like His Word).

When we talk about, meditate on, and delight in the things God loves, and give glory to Him, I imagine He delights too. In fact, Psalm 116:2 says He, "bends down to hear our prayer." This sounds just like a parent bending down to make sure they understand every word their child says.

Many times Emilio has to ask me to interpret for him what Eden is saying, and I'm honored to know her so well that I can discern almost all her words. God knows His children like that. He knows our thoughts before we speak them (Psalm 139:2b) and knows our sitting down and rising up (Psalm 139:2a). He is familiar with all our ways (Just read all of Psalm 139. You'll be glad you did). I know when Eden rises and goes to bed, when she first stood and when she first sat, and I still love to see her do those things.

As I was putting her to bed and singing words from Psalm 119, which I have done many times, a specific part comforted me in a new way. The words in verse 90 say, "Your faithfulness continues throughout all generations." That is profoundly comforting that He won't leave Eden's generation. We have His Word that He is faithful in every generation. That should be a soft pillow for us to sleep on.

May the Lord direct your hearts into the love of God and into the steadfastness of Christ.

2 Thessalonians 3:5

☞ PATIENCE ☜

We proclaim Him, admonishing every man and teaching every man with all wisdom, so that we may present every man complete in Christ.

Colossians 1:28

$\mathcal{M}$ARCH 19, 2019

Eden has become very picky about her food. She wants to eat what SHE wants to eat. And I get it. I can be like that too, but it's gotten her into some constipation trouble because she is not eating a lot of fruit and veggies or drinking enough water. I think it's having its toll. So I pray for her, and she even asks me to pray for her.

This reminds me of the time I lived on my own at age 19. I vividly remember being afraid my first night alone. I was staying in a large two-story condo type apartment, which was empty except for my bedroom furniture. The first night by myself the power was accidentally shut off. We didn't have cell phones then, so I had to drive to a pay phone blocks away late at night. Talk about frazzled nerves. My poor mom was mortified when she heard the power was off. Turns out, it was a mistake on the part of the power company that was resolved quickly. All that to say, I was young and not used to doing things like this for myself, and I didn't realize just how much my mom did for me. I'm eternally grateful for her and all she did while growing up.

For instance, my mom graciously made me meals that were balanced and healthy, and I never had any health issues. I don't know how she did all that she did. She worked and made sure I was fed and clean and dressed, and our home was immaculate. She would always make sure that my meals consisted of meat, a carb of some sort and a vegetable. But after they moved away, my eating became disjointed, and I developed an eating disorder (properly called an eating sin, not a disorder, as the world labels it). Shortly thereafter, I developed hypothyroidism. I didn't know what was wrong with me though and continued going to get blood work but everything always looked normal. However, I was very, very sick; almost dead. When I was at the doctor for an annual physical about 5 years after the eating sins, he came into the room and looked like he saw a ghost. He said, "Your thyroid is not working, and you should be a lot heavier than you are and I'm not sure how you are functioning at all. I'm very sorry." He looked scared for me, but I was just glad to finally have a diagnosis. I almost leapt for joy when I left the room. I had been praying for God to help me.

The doctor put me on a high dose of thyroid medicine. Fifteen years later, I'm still on it, but by God's grace, I've been able to reduce the dosage by half. It has not been easy getting to this point. For the past four years, I've had to go gluten-free, dairy-free, oat-free, egg-free and soy-free. If I eat just one egg or oatmeal cookie, my face will break out. If I eat any gluten or dairy, I have to increase my thyroid medication. My health issues have all been a lesson that there are consequences to sin.

For years, I thought I could abuse my body and not pay for it, but God's Word is right. Galatians 6:8 says, "For the one who sows to his own flesh will from the flesh reap corruption, but the one who sows to the Spirit will from the Spirit reap eternal life."

Keep reading though, verse 9 says, "Let us not lose heart in doing good, for in due time we will reap if we do not grow weary." If verse 8 is true, and it is, then so is verse 9. We must believe that. We are told that in due time we will reap if we do not grow weary. And, boy, do I want to sow to the Spirit more than ever as I see the days growing shorter and increasingly dark.

Our missionary friend, Josef Urban, told me something that reminds me of Galatians 6:9. He said something to the effect of "everything you put in your body today will have an effect on you within a decade." And that "every nine months our body regenerates." What a thought, especially if you are attempting to cure your body of disease. It will take a lot of time, but good things can come to those who wait.

> "Wait for the LORD; Be strong and let your heart take courage; Yes, wait for the LORD." Psalm 27:14

> "Surely none who wait for You will be put to shame; but those who are faithless without cause will be disgraced." Psalm 25:3

> "Be strong and courageous, all you who hope in the LORD." Psalm 31:24

> "Wait for the LORD and keep His way, and He will raise you up to inherit the land. When the wicked are cut off, you will see it." Psalm 37:34

> "I waited patiently for the LORD; He inclined to me and heard my cry." Psalm 40:1

> "Rest in God alone, O my soul, for my hope comes from Him." Psalm 62:5

> "I wait for the LORD; my soul does wait, and in His Word I put my hope." Psalm 130:5

My prayer is that Eden Joy will not battle issues with food as many have, including Eve. It was Eve's desire for food that got her in much trouble. May Eden have a different spirit. May God help our children to live for Him at early ages.

After writing today's entry, I noticed a text from a friend. It was very fitting with what I had just written, so I thought I'd include it. It's taken from Charles Spurgeon, Morning and Evening:

"And she did eat, and was sufficed, (satisfied) and left." (Ruth 2:14) Whenever we are privileged to eat of the bread which Jesus gives, we are, like Ruth, satisfied with the full and sweet repast. When Jesus is the host, no guest goes empty from the table. Our head is satisfied with the precious truth, which Christ reveals; our heart is content with Jesus, as the altogether lovely object of affection; our hope is satisfied, for whom have we in heaven but Jesus? And our desire is satiated, for what can we wish for more than "to know Christ and to be found in him?" Jesus fills our conscience till it is at perfect peace; our judgment with persuasion of the certainty of his teachings; our memory with recollections of what he has done, and our imagination with the prospects of what he is yet to do. As Ruth was "sufficed, and left," so is it with us. We have had deep draughts; we have thought that we could take in all of Christ; but when we have done our best we have had to leave a vast remainder. We have sat at the table of the Lord's love, and said, "Nothing but the infinite can ever satisfy me; I am such a great sinner that I must have infinite merit to wash my sin away;" but we have had our sin removed, and found that there was merit to spare; we have had our hunger relieved at the feast of sacred love, and found that there was a redundancy of spiritual meat remaining. There are certain sweet things in the Word of God which we have not enjoyed yet, and which we are obliged to leave for a while; for we are like the disciples to whom Jesus said, "I have yet many things to say unto you, but ye cannot bear them now." Yes, there are graces to which we have not attained; places of fellowship nearer to Christ which we have not reached; and heights of communion which our feet have not climbed. At every banquet of love, there are many baskets of fragments left. Let us magnify the liberality of our glorious Boaz.

We proclaim Him, admonishing every man and teaching every man with all wisdom, so that we may present every man complete in Christ.

Colossians 1:28

❧ WORSHIP ☙

O LORD, how many are Your works! In wisdom You have made them all; The earth is full of Your possessions.

Psalm 104:24

𝓜 ARCH 20, 2019

I stayed home almost the whole day, spending most of it in Eden's room playing, worshipping, coloring, dancing, reading, singing and watching birds out the window. It was great, like a small taste of heaven. I pretended for a short while that all was well in the world, while Eden pretended to do my hair and get me ready for a wedding we are going to this weekend. I felt like I was at the salon (which I have only been to a handful of times in my life), and could have easily fallen asleep. Instead, I decided to turn on an old album called *Wow Worship*.

One song on *Wow Worship* has the lyrics,

"Blessing and honor, glory and power be unto the Ancient of Days

All of creation, from every nation, will bow before the Ancient of Days

Every tongue in heaven and earth will declare Your glory,

Every knee will bow at Your throne and worship

You will be exalted Oh God, and Your Kingdom shall
not pass away, oh Ancient of Days."

Eden loves that song. I used to play it when I first got
saved, and it was nice to have her join me in remembering
such a special time.

I pulled up the window blinds so we could see the
sunshine and look at the people walking their pets outside. Eden put her hands on the window and began calling out to a lonesome blackbird on our front lawn. She
really wanted it to hear her. Then it flew away, and she
looked over her shoulder at me with her big eyes and said
"Mama, can you pray it comes back?" I said, "Of course,"
and prayed, "Lord if it would please you, please bring that
bird or another for us to delight in. You know the path of
the birds, and you can direct them to us, Amen." Then I
stood up and told her I would be on the "lookout for birds
to return should God decide to bring them." And before
I could lift my eyes to scan our yard, I saw two doves sitting on our wall right next to the window. God answered
our prayer before we even prayed. This reminded me of
the reference to the new heavens and new earth in Isaiah
65:24: "It will also come to pass that before they call, I
will answer; and while they are still speaking, I will hear."
What a day to look forward to!

O LORD, how many are Your works! In wisdom You have made them all; The earth is full of Your possessions.

Psalm 104:24

☙ PROVISION ❧

Now may our Lord Jesus Christ Himself and God our Father, who has loved us and given us eternal comfort and good hope by grace, comfort and strengthen your hearts in every good work and word.

2 Thessalonians 2:16-17

*M*ARCH 21, 2019

Today a friend from church (Kim) came over to do some decorating in my entryway. I wanted to be surprised, so Eden and I went on a walk with Kim's children while she decorated. As we headed out, the two doves I talked about yesterday were out again. Eden and I had seen them earlier in our backyard as well, basking in the spring sunlight. It reminded me of when Jesus said to "look at the birds" in Matthew 6:26, which is incredibly easy to do when He puts them right in your yard two days in a row.

Kim had everything ready for the big reveal as soon as we returned from walking. Her decorating was beyond lovely. My eyes were darting everywhere taking it all in, but what caught my attention most were two little white birds on the ledge of my niche. Not only were they a perfect reminder of the doves Eden and I had been delighting in, but they also served as a reminder of God's provision and kindness...that if He takes care of the birds, He will take care of us. "Look at the birds of the air, that they do not sow, nor reap nor gather into barns, and yet your heavenly

Father feeds them. Are you not worth much more than they?" (Matthew 6:26)

I wonder if Eden will remember the doves, or any of these things that I've written about, seeing as she is so young. If not, at least they are written down for her to read later, which reminds me of Malachi 3:16 that says: "Then those who feared the Lord spoke to one another, and the Lord gave attention and heard it, *and a book of remembrance was written before Him for those who fear the Lord and who esteem His name.*"

God invented journaling (if you will) and book writing. Remember, He is the author of the greatest book ever written. And what's amazing about Malachi's verse is that it is a book written especially *for* those who fear the name of the Lord. Amazing, indeed.

Now may our Lord Jesus Christ Himself and God our Father, who has loved us and given us eternal comfort and good hope by grace, comfort and strengthen your hearts in every good work and word.

2 Thessalonians 2:16-17

❧ EXPRESSION ❧

Only conduct yourselves in a manner worthy of the gospel of Christ, so that whether I come and see you or remain absent, I will hear of you that you are standing firm in one spirit, with one mind striving together for the faith of the gospel;

Philippians 1:27

*M*ARCH 23, 2019

Our family went to a wedding today.

The wedding was being held an hour from our home, and we were late getting there. Not because we left late, as Emilio doesn't like ever to be late for anything, we actually left right on time for a 2:00 wedding. But it turns out the wedding was at 1:30.

The wedding was short and must have started promptly at 1:30 because when we arrived, it was over. Thankfully, the groom's pastor was officiating, not Emilio. He has done many weddings and funerals and has never missed one. I'm glad he showed up for our wedding.

However, Emilio did have a short time allotted during the ceremony to preach the gospel (the groom's pastor ended up doing it). Emilio went up to the pastor immediately after we arrived, explained the situation and apologized. The pastor had a great attitude about it, and Emilio said, "Well, I guess God wants you to be ready *in season and out.*"

The pastor laughed and said, "That is the exact verse I'll be preaching tomorrow for my Sunday message."

The icing on the (wedding) cake happened on the ride home. We were all in the car when out of the blue Eden said, "Jesse got married, and ladies were serving cake like Jesus." She had pieced together my talks with her about Jesus serving us at the marriage supper of the Lamb, and seeing some of the bridal party serve cake to the guest. Her comment surprised all of us and made me realize that we can't begin speaking God's Word to our children too soon. I think from birth is a good time to start. When Eden was born, I threw my right arm in the air and yelled out "Jesus is King!" And Emilio said to her, "Jesus is Lord." It's never too late to start, and then continue, talking to your children about all God has done…in season and out.

After the wedding, Eden laid on her back for a long time and let me talk to her. It was a sweet time as it reminded me of when she was a little baby. We talked a lot about the Lord. At one point I showed her a lotion bottle with a drawing of a baby on it. She looked at it and said, "I don't like that baby."

I asked her why, but she didn't have an answer. All she said was, "Well...I just want milk." How much she understands what she's saying, I'm not sure, but maybe a lot more than I think. I told her Pharaoh did not like babies and asked her if she wanted to be like him, to which she clearly said no. Then I told her how Jesus loved children and asked if she wanted to be like him and she said yes.

I said that God would help her heart in that area. She even asked me to pray for that.

Where she is getting not liking babies from (other than her sinful nature), I don't know. I pray God will instead put in her a care, love and desire for them. That she will one day have several of her own, for her joy and delight.

One more thing before bed, I saw this post on Facebook that a member of our church shared from "Above Rubies" page that is convicting and encouraging:

WHAT DO THEY SEE?

I don't think there is anything more beautiful than a mother looking with adoration at her baby. Even a plain mother is beautiful when she looks lovingly at her child. Jean Millet writes: "Beauty does not lie in the face. Beauty is expression. When I paint a mother, I try to render her beautiful by the mere look she gives her child."

It truly is the expression of our face that is beautiful to the beholder. It is our expression that comes from within that makes us beautiful or otherwise. I am always challenged by the words in Isaiah 3:9: "The show of their countenance doth witness against them." Isn't it so true? Our countenance gives us away. It reveals what's on the inside.

Let's keep a good attitude. Cast aside all negativity, anger, hurt, bitterness, unforgiveness and let's fill our lies with the beauty of forgiveness, love, joy, and unselfishness.

2 Corinthians 3:18 tells us how that when we behold the face of Jesus, we are changed into His likeness. This also happens with us and our children. Our children behold our face all day long. What do they see? An expression of contentment and joy? Or frustration and anger? A smile or a frown?

Dear mother, your children will change into the same image they see on your face. Do you want happy, smiling children? Let them see this expression on your face.

I love the words of the hymn:

> *Let the beauty of Jesus be seen in me,*
> *All his wonderful passion and purity,*
> *O thou Spirit divine, all my nature refine,*
> *Till the beauty of Jesus be seen in me.*

May the expression on our faces make us look beautiful to our husbands and children.

Only conduct yourselves in a manner worthy of the gospel of Christ, so that whether I come and see you or remain absent, I will hear of you that you are standing firm in one spirit, with one mind striving together for the faith of the gospel;

Philippians 1:27

❥ RESCUER ❦

God is a Spirit, and they that worship him must worship him in spirit and in truth.

John 4:24

*M*ARCH 24, 2019

Parenting can sometimes include moments we would like to forget, which reminds me of an event I read about this morning. The title said...

"Norway Cruise Ship Evacuated After Engine Problems"

The BBC article read:

"Rescue crews worked through the night on Saturday to rescue 1,300 people stranded on a cruise ship off the west coast of Norway...

Norway's sea rescue agency said the MV Viking Sky sent out a distress signal amid high waves and strong winds.

Five helicopters and several rescue ships were called in for the rescue.

One of the rescue ships—a freighter named Hagland Captain—also lost engine power and two helicopters were diverted to rescue its crew.

By Sunday morning, the ship had managed to restart three of its four engines and was attempting to move closer to the nearest port.

'We were having lunch when [the ship] began to shake,' John Curry, who was evacuated by helicopter, told public broadcaster NRK. 'Window panes were broken, and water came in. It was just chaos. The trip on the helicopter, I would rather forget. It was not fun,' he said.

Janet Jacob, who was also rescued, told the channel she had 'never seen anything so frightening.'"

Parenting can sometimes feel like a cruise ship gone bad. One minute you're dancing, laughing and playing and the next you are pleading with God for help because your attitude or your child's attitude is sinking.

"I started to pray. I prayed for the safety of everyone on board," one lady aboard the ship said. "The helicopter trip was terrifying."

The article said only a handful of people were injured, thankfully.

If you are a parent, no doubt you've had the time when you're busy in the kitchen and were not as patient as you should have been and injured someone's heart. Or perhaps in the car, someone cut you off, and you lost your witness in front of your child. Or maybe you've been tested with your child's rebellion, and you didn't exhibit the kind and patient instruction and discipline that you should have. Whatever the "wreck" you have found yourself in, the good news is we have a Father who bends His ear to hear and is quick to rescue and forgive.

I think of all the manpower that has gone underway to help the 1,300 people off the Viking ship. Man sure has gone to great lengths to help man.

And God has gone to greater lengths to help man, namely, sending Christ to rescue and deliver us from our sin. What a rescue team we have!

Not to mention the rescue team we have in the church body that encourages and edifies us. For some reason though, it's been hard for me to get to church lately. It's like I drag my feet going (probably because my thyroid medicine is low), but I always leave clicking my heels.

My mom can attest to that too. She said she was downcast for some reason yesterday, but today's sermon helped lift it. Praise God.

After church, we went home, and I spent a lot of time just enjoying and watching Eden play. It was nice. She loves to wash her dolls and really anything she can grab, like Mickey or Minnie Mouse or her mama or baby rabbit. Then, she did something new. She put her shoes on by herself. Her clear sparkle-toe jelly ones. I didn't see her do it, I just heard Emilio from around the corner say, "You put them on the wrong feet." And I thought, "What?! She did what?!" I told him not to encourage her in this new endeavor. I want to put her shoes on her for another year or longer (or the rest of her life!).

We also did some family worship tonight before bed. Emilio played guitar, I did the shaker, and Eden grabbed her little guitar and started playing very seriously. Handling all the cuteness was hard. Then she turned to Emilio and said, "Can you not play so loud?" And told me to turn my shaker "off." She cracks me up.

As I was holding her for bedtime, I sang, "Our sins they are many, His mercy is more. Praise the Lord oh-oh His mercies are more oh-oh. Stronger than darkness new every morn...our sins they are many, His mercy is more." I had my eyes closed singing that one stanza over and over, all the while thinking Eden's eyes were closed too. When I looked down though, she had her hand raised as if to worship. Oh, how I pray for a heart of worship for Eden, for your children, and for each one of us.

Lord, we confess You are good, and we are not. We acknowledge that we need Your help even to worship You. Would you put songs on our heart in the morning and the evening and all throughout the day? Do the same for our children. Please cause them to be true worshippers, by Your power. Amen.

I played "Is He Worthy?" by Chris Tomlin before bed too.

Eden said, "Is Mama Worthy?" Then she shook her head as to say no.

She asked if Papa was "worthy" and if Meesie and Ompiee (her grandparents) were "worthy" as well? Again shaking her head as to say no.

Then she did something surprising. She shot her arm straight in the air and said, "Only Jesus!" while nodding her head as to say yes. I just started crying. She took her little hands and dried the tears off my face.

He is indeed worthy!

"Praise the Lord, my soul; all my inmost being, praise His holy name." (Psalm 103:1)

"My mouth is filled with your praise, declaring your splendor all day long." (Psalm 71:8)

"Yours, Lord, is the greatness and the power and the glory and the majesty and the splendor, for everything in heaven and earth is yours. Yours, Lord, is the kingdom; you are exalted as head over all." (1 Chronicles 29:11)

"How great you are, Sovereign Lord! There is no one like you, and there is no God but you, as we have heard with our own ears." (2 Samuel 7:22)

"There is no one holy like the Lord; there is no one besides you; there is no Rock like our God." (1 Samuel 2:2)

God is a Spirit, and they that worship him must worship him in spirit and in truth.

John 4:24

❧ PRESENCE ❦

Yes, and I will rejoice, for I know that this will turn out for my deliverance through your prayers and the provision of the Spirit of Jesus Christ…

Philippians 1:18b-19

*M*ARCH 25, 2019

Last night I prayed about singing, that Eden and the children of all of you reading this would sing for God. Just the thought brought me much joy. But this morning I find myself downcast because of a headache in my left temple. I've been battling this pain for four days, and I am certain my thyroid medication is the cause. It is either too high or too low. Sometimes it's tricky because if you are too high in medicine you can have a headache and if you are too low, you can as well. I don't wish a thyroid problem on my worst enemy.

In light of this, I didn't talk a lot today, which is not normal, so Eden did the talking for both of us. And she sang songs throughout the day. It was a pleasant, momentary distraction from the thorn in my flesh and made me think that I should talk less to see what she will say.

First, she sang, "Jesus loves me" and "Joy to the World." Then "Undignified" by Matt Redman, singing the words, "I will dance, I will sing, to be mad for my King…I'll become even more undignified than this." I was amazed at

Eden's song choices as none of them were prompted by me and I don't remember the last time we listened to any of those.

Did you know that both Eden's first and middle name (Joy) are in the Bible in one verse, Isaiah 51:3?

"Indeed the Lord will comfort Zion. He will comfort all her waste places and her wilderness he will make like Eden and her deserts like the garden of the Lord. Joy and gladness will be round in her thanksgiving and the sound of a melody (or the sound of music)."

Like the verse says, may the sound of a melody and singing always be on her heart like it was today.

Before bed, Eden had a handheld fan that she wouldn't put down. It's pretty as it lights up with the words "Rejoice in the Lord" all in red. She looked at it told me "Jesus would like this." I was reminded, after she put the fan in front of my face several times and kept saying it, that God wants me to rejoice in Him. Eden had to say it over and over. I'm slow sometimes. Really slow.

Paul did the same thing to the church in Philippians when he said over and over, "Rejoice in the Lord always; again I will say, rejoice!" (Philippians 4:4)

In fact, God tells us to rejoice over and over throughout His Word. Here are just a few verses:

"Rejoice in the LORD, O you righteous; befitting is the praise of the upright." (Psalm 33:1)

"Yet I will exult in the LORD; I will rejoice in the God of my salvation!" Habakkuk 3:18

"...as sorrowful, yet always rejoicing; poor, yet making many rich; having nothing, and yet possessing everything." (2 Corinthians 6:10)

"Finally, my brothers, rejoice in the Lord. It is no trouble for me to write the same things to you again, and it is a safeguard for you." (Philippians 3:1)

"Rejoice at all times." (1 Thessalonians 5:16)

That last verse is short and good, but oh, so hard at times.

Speaking of repeating things, maybe some of you have heard of Tony Miano. He used to work for Ray Comfort at The Way of the Master TV show when I worked there several years ago.

I came to know recently that Tony hand writes letters to people that request them during his free time, especially those in need of ministering. As I was reading testimonies about his handwritten letters I wanted one too. So I wrote to him.

Days later, a three-page letter arrived in my mailbox in the most perfect handwriting. In fact, the writing was so perfect and so beautiful that I kept checking it to see if it was printed from a computer. My mom's writing is perfect and beautiful much like his.

In the letter, Tony talked about Philippians 4.

"Rejoice in the Lord always; again I will say, rejoice. Let your reasonableness be known to everyone. The Lord is at hand; do not be anxious about anything, but in everything by prayer and supplication with thanksgiving let your requests be made known to God. And the peace of God, which surpasses all understanding, will guard your hearts and your minds in Christ Jesus" (Philippians 4:4-7).

I thought to myself I know this passage. I've even memorized it.

Tony repeated several times the phrase "The Lord is at hand." And by the fifth time, I got it. It's like I got hit upside the head. I always thought that verse was talking about the second coming of Christ. At least in my mind, that is where I always tend to go. As if to say, "get ready the Lord is coming (He is at hand)." Which is a true statement, but it seems the Lord is saying something more intimate and personal in this particular verse.

Tony said it appears to be more like "the Lord is ever present" and near us, and he backed up his reasons.

I studied it further, and tonight I read an article by Sam Storms titled, "THE LORD IS AT HAND! NO, IT'S NOT THE SECOND COMING":

It made me laugh that it was in all capital letters. Sam Storms says, in some very timely and comforting words,

> "This phrase 'at hand' could be taken temporally or personally. That is to say, he may be referring to the nearness of Christ in terms of time or space. If it's time, he may be alluding back to what he said at the close of chapter three. There we were encouraged to keep our eyes fixed on heaven from which 'we await a Savior, the Lord Jesus Christ' (3:20b).
>
> But I'm inclined to think he is speaking in spatial or relational or personal terms. His point, then, is that the Lord is close to you, present with you, aware of your conduct, concerned about your relationships with others, available and willing to come to your aid and assist you. This may well be why Paul immediately follows this declaration with an important command that we pray. If the Lord is near to help and encourage and strengthen us, we need to be quick to pray to him about everything! We hear an echo of this

in Psalm 145:18 – 'The Lord is near to all who call on him, to all who call on him in truth.'"

How encouraging to know all my concerns in life, and with Eden, I can cast on the Lord, who is near and always at hand. He is not far off. Just like I never want to be far off from Eden. I want to hear her requests and be available to answer and help. So it is with our great King.

Yes, and I will rejoice, for I know that this will turn out for my deliverance through your prayers and the provision of the Spirit of Jesus Christ...

Philippians 1:18b-19

❧ LATE ☙

She senses that her gain is good; Her lamp does not go out at night.

Proverbs 31:18

M
ARCH 26, 2019

Emilio told me that people who rise early and go to bed early tend to live longer. At least that is what some studies show. I tend to stay up quite late to get things done around the house and to write. Emilio made this comment to me at about 3am, so you get an idea of what my "late" looks like.

I responded back to him saying, "Well, my Bible tells me that the Proverbs 31 woman's lamp does not go out at night.

He said, "Oh wow. That's a good one."

She senses that her gain is good; Her lamp does not go out at night.

Proverbs 31:18

❧ THANKFUL ❧

Looking for the blessed hope and the appearing of the glory of our great God and Savior, Christ Jesus…

Titus 2:13a

MARCH 27, 2019

Today was one of those days where it seemed that everything I touched went south. I battled fatigue, another headache in my left temple and ringing in my ears. I didn't have the vision I usually do when I play with and teach Eden. At one point, I decided to push through it all and throw Eden around a bit on my knees and have fun, and ended up throwing out my shoulder and neck. To get my mind off all my health woes, I thought it best to think of those things that happened today that I'm thankful for. During Eden's nap I typed these things on my phone (as I was not feeling well at all, and wrote this in faith):

Thank you Lord that…

- We completed all shredding (grateful for a small task done).

- Eden got to paint outside with me for the first time ever. I put her in a red t-shirt of mine that she could get dirty. She said, "We match." I hadn't even noticed I was wearing the same color sweater.

- Yesterday my heart was fluttering a lot. Today it is not. Thank you, Lord.

- A friend called and throughout our very brief conversation kept saying, "Rejoice in the Lord." I laughed as it finally hit me that she was probably referencing my post from the day before yesterday about Eden and her fan that says, "Rejoice in the Lord." But she said that she had no idea what I was talking about. So I learned another lesson, that God is still trying to teach me to rejoice in Him, not in my health or how I feel, but only in Him.

- Listened to worship on a nice walk around the block with Eden as she smelled the neighbor's flowers, and accidentally picked one. We knocked on the neighbor's door just to let her know why we were on her lawn and in her flowerbed. She didn't seem too happy, but she did smile and tell us to go ahead. She told me she was working and pointed to her office window right where we were standing. She was probably watching us the whole time. I'd better go back with a new plant and tracts and maybe a sweet treat to redeem the picked flower situation.

- Meditated on Psalm 72, which is oh, so good, specifically verse 12, "For He will deliver the needy when he cries for help, The afflicted also, and him who has no helper." What a hopeful verse. There are three individual conditions mentioned in it, the needy, the afflicted, and him who has no helper. Maybe you are one of those three. Or all three, if you are like me. The key word in the passage is "deliver." God is going to do that one thing for all three situations. Amen.

Looking for the blessed hope and the appearing of the glory of our great God and Savior, Christ Jesus...

Titus 2:13a

❧ APPOINTMENTS ❧

> *"Therefore He is able also to save forever those who draw near to God through Him, since He always lives to make intercession for them."*
>
> Hebrews 7:25

*M*ARCH 28, 2019

Remind me to never leave the house without taking gospel tracts with me. Yesterday was difficult health-wise, but I managed to drag my body out and run a couple errands by evening. It turned out to be a very encouraging time. Here's why...

I stopped at Lowe's to get some double-sided tape and asked a worker named Jackie for help finding it. She told me it was on aisle 7. I thanked her and handed her an invitation to our church. The invitation is simply a business-sized card with our church information on the front and the gospel on the back; it's both beautiful and to the point. When I gave it to her, I said, "This is for you if you have nowhere to go on Sunday. You can even sleep in because our service starts at 2:30." That seems to give everyone a good laugh. She said, "You know what, I think you came this way for a reason. I've been looking for a church."

I was really blessed to hear her say that, and for just a moment, forgot how terrible I felt.

Upon leaving the store, I spotted a young man walking in and said, "Here...this is for you if you don't have anywhere to go on Sunday."

He said, "Well thank you...I've actually been looking for a church."

I said, "What? I mean, are you related to Jackie who works here because she just told me the same thing and you both look alike?"

He said, "Nope. I don't have any relatives that work here."

I chuckled inside thinking of the kindness of the Lord to do this.

Then I headed to Sprouts, and was in the organic vegetable aisle when I heard a man say, "Nice shirt."

I had to look down to remind myself that I was wearing a shirt that says "Salvation" on the front and "3:16" on the sleeve.

I gave him some gospel tracts and learned that he was moving from California to Texas from the same area where our family had moved. I gave him an invitation to church too.

None of these encounters took much time (If I tallied them all up they took maybe five minutes), but they brought so much encouragement. I thank God that He didn't design evangelism for the unbelievers good only, but for the believers good as well!

If you have never handed out a gospel tract, I urge you to do it. LivingWaters.com has packs of 100 tracts for the price of a cup of coffee. Buying just one pack of tracts will enable you to touch 100 souls that will, in turn, touch yours somehow. Even getting rejected is for your good too. Romans 8:28 says so.

You will thank me in heaven.

Right before publishing this book, I sent my sister-in-law, Miriam, an excerpt to read. Here is her reply:

"Thank you, Trish, for this.

For sharing your heart and thoughts with me, and others.

So many people are in the same place you know... in different ways, but still struggling for joy.

And all the verses are fitting for everyone...no matter the struggle or thorn in our flesh. We need to seek the Father more often than we do...like Jesus did, and was always aware that the Father was right there. There was no second thought of that reality.

We have a compassionate God...and yet we want to carry the load...when we can't do a single thing apart from Him.

Even joy is from God.

John 16.24 says, 'Until now you have asked nothing in my name. Ask, and you will receive, that your joy may be full.'

Children are also a means of God's work in our sanctification...not just for learning patience... many parents know that truth...but a bigger truth is that God's purposes are higher than ours."

Such truth Miriam imparted. We can't carry the load. We weren't even *designed* to. And our merciful Jesus says to "come to Him all who are weary, and he will give us rest." (Matthew 11:28)

Rest yourself tonight saint and sister. Let your head rest on the soft pillow of God's grace and peace.

"Therefore He is able also to save forever those who draw near to God through Him, since He always lives to make intercession for them."

Hebrews 7:25

❥ FOCUS ❧

Blessed be the God and Father of our Lord Jesus Christ, who has blessed us with every spiritual blessing in the heavenly places in Christ…

Ephesians 1:3

MARCH 29, 2019

We had some trouble getting out of the house today. Eden didn't want to wear pants, which was making us late in getting blood work done for my thyroid. Finally, we made it out the door, only to get lost driving to the clinic. I said a prayer out loud for God to help us, and we eventually found our destination.

We walked into the clinic and met our technician who was from another country. I thought perhaps Serbia, but he said he was from Macedonia. He looked at Eden and said, "My daughter is five."

"How nice," I said. "What is her name?"

"Ellie," he said.

His answer reminded me that Eden often prays that I will have a baby named "Ellie." Which then made me think of Romans 8:28, how "God causes all things to work together for good to those who love God, to those who are called according to His purpose." My afternoon had started off frustrating, but God was indeed turning it to good, starting with giving our technician one of our church tracts.

After the clinic, we stopped for an ice cream, passed out more tracts and walked around The Star, which is where the Dallas Cowboys train. We walked into a store to give tracts to the workers, and one said, "We have apple juice here, can I make her a cup?" I thought, "It's nice to walk around with Eden. We give out free things, and we get free things." It turned out to be a fine day.

Eventually, we headed home, and in the car we were singing, "The B-I-B-L-E, yes, that's the book for me!" and "Hark the Herald," when Eden started to complain that her seat belt was uncomfortable. I told her that we are almost home, and I was not crazy about my seatbelt either. I tried to take her mind off of her seat belt by doing a little puppet show with a stuffed rabbit while we were sitting at a red light (that felt like it was taking forever). I handed it to her, and she said, "I do not love you." I thought she was saying that to the rabbit, but turns out she was saying it to me (wow, being a mom is full of ups and downs and highs and lows). Looks like "*Struggles and Sunshine Part 2*" will be coming out sooner than I thought.

Let's purpose today to fix out eyes on Jesus (Who doesn't not change). Who is the same, today, tomorrow and forever (Hebrews 13:8).

Blessed be the God and Father of our Lord Jesus Christ, who has blessed us with every spiritual blessing in the heavenly places in Christ...

Ephesians 1:3

⪼ KING ⪻

*The next day John saw Jesus coming toward him and said,
"Look, the Lamb of God, who takes away the sin of the
world!"*

John 1:29

*A*pril 1, 2019

Eden woke up today singing, "Worship the King."

That's all I needed today.

Let's do that today. Worship Him, period.

*The next day John saw Jesus coming toward him and said,
"Look, the Lamb of God, who takes away the sin of the
world!"*

John 1:29

ᦠ RADIANCE ᦡ

*They looked to Him and were radiant, and their faces will
never be ashamed.*

Psalm 34:5

*A*pril 5, 2019

Eden has been battling constipation again.

Part of me thinks she might be afraid to go, so she gets
backed up. While another part of me thinks it has to do
with her wanting control over what she eats.

So I'm going to try something new. I'm going to place
in front of her the foods that I want her to eat. If she re-
fuses them, she can eat later, but it will be the same foods.
At that point, I'll tell her, "This is the food God that has
provided for us right now." I pray it doesn't turn into a
big battle between her and me, but that she will come to
realize that these foods are for her benefit.

In addition to Eden's constipation returning, my headache in my temple area returned, right after I ate some
yogurt. I've been dairy-free for a long time because of
my Hashimoto's Thyroiditis but thought it would be no
big deal to eat two yogurts as a treat. Boy, was I wrong.
This headache has been a nagging enemy for two weeks,
a complete thorn in the flesh causing me to fight hard
for joy. Some days it's been challenging to pull out of a
grumbling spirit, and at times I think Eden picks up on
it. Even though I'm not complaining outwardly, my heart
inwardly is grumbling.

Like today in the car, she said, "Mama, are you upset?"

"No, you silly goose," I told her.

She said, "Are you frustrated?"

"No, you silly goose."

How does she even know the word frustrated?

I just changed the subject and did a little puppet show in the backseat for her, and all was well.

It's amazing how well she knows me and picks up on things.

This all happened on the way to the thyroid doctor to get results for my blood work. My numbers are indeed off a bit, which explains my headache and why my usual dose of thyroid medicine wasn't working. I've learned in the past that the dairy from the yogurt clogs the liver making thyroid medicine less potent. So, no more yogurt for me, again.

As we were leaving the doctor, I gave a tract to a man and his wife. The man smiled from ear to ear as he took it. He looked like he was from Zimbabwe, where I traveled to in 1997 to reach people for Christ.

Eden said, "Mama, I like his demeanor."

I couldn't believe my ears.

It was so precious to hear her say that.

I plead with God that He will give all of us moms demeanors that our children like. That He will shine on us, and we will be as radiant as that man's smile.

Perhaps we need to "look to Him" more. I know I do. His Word says, "They looked to Him and were radiant, and their faces will never be ashamed." (Psalm 34:5)

I need to tape that verse on my mirror and pin it on the door of my heart.

May God help us to parent with joy and instruct with joy, even when we don't feel well. That this kind of instruction will come to us naturally because of Who we serve; the Source of all joy. That we will delight in our children delighting in things and other people, even when we feel discarded and left out and un-thanked.

The only thing that seemed to pull me out of my inward grumbling today was meditating on Philippians 2, specifically, verses 14 and 15:

"Do all things without grumbling or disputing; so that you will prove yourselves to be blameless and innocent, children of God above reproach in the midst of a crooked and perverse generation, among whom you appear as lights in the world."

What powerful truth.

Are you doing all things without grumbling and complaining? I don't know about you, but I certainly don't want to be like the children of Israel that were disciplined for grumbling and complaining. (Numbers 11:1) Let's aim this week to try to master that and put to death what is "earthly" in us (Colossians 3).

Every time you are tempted to grumble, quote this to yourself: "Do all things without grumbling and complaining."

Lord, we confess that You are strong, and we are not. Fill us with your Spirit and empower us to do what we cannot do, for we cannot do anything apart from You. Put smiles on our faces, making them radiant for Your glory and our children's good. Amen.

They looked to Him and were radiant, and their faces will never be ashamed.

Psalm 34:5

So then, while we have opportunity, let us do good to all people, and especially to those who are of the household of the faith.

Galatians 6:10

*A*pril 8, 2019

Someone sent us in the mail the most adorable spoons and we don't even know who they are from...they just put the letter "C" when signing the card. Whoever you are... we thank you!

The spoons say "Be brave and keep strong" and "He Gives Me Joy."

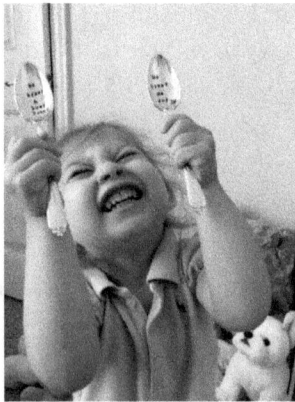

So then, while we have opportunity, let us do good to all people, and especially to those who are of the household of the faith.

Galatians 6:10

CROSS

Out of the mouths of nursing babes and infants He has perfected praise.

Psalm 8:2

*A*pril 10, 2019

Eden has a book by R.C. Sproul called "The Donkey Who Carried a King." I read it to her when she was about 6 months old and I wept. And recently I showed her the book and got to the page where all you see is an angry mob and part of the cross sticking up. You can't see the Lord but you can tell someone is carrying it. I asked her what it was? And I made her think a long time about it. And then I told her. She seemed really touched by it. This must have been a few months ago. Then today while outside she saw a piece of bark on the ground from our flowerbed and said, "Mama that looks like the cross Jesus carried." I was blown away. Then she began to describe what happened and that the cross was "much too heavy for Him to carry." I couldn't handle how precious this was and how adorable her hands looked as she told me. I recorded it on my phone. And posted it online and many people were touched and it received a lot of views. I'm sure the angles in heaven were enjoying hearing her as well.

Out of the mouths of nursing babes and infants He has perfected praise.

Psalm 8:2

❧ SWEETNESS ❧

Who redeems your life from the pit, Who crowns you with loving kindness and tender mercies.

Psalm 103:4

*A*pril 12, 2019

Before bed tonight Eden said, "You know what, mama, I love you and you are special to me." Then she said, "Let me have your hand." And she held my hand and gave me a kiss on it.

Thank you Lord for this sweetness. Thank you for allowing me to live to see such kind things in this dark world. Spare Eden's soul, dear Lord, for Your names sake, for my joy and the joy of all who know her.

Who redeems your life from the pit, Who crowns you with loving kindness and tender mercies

Psalm 103:4

❧ SONGS ☙

Whatever you do, whether you eat or drink, do all to the glory of God.

1 Corinthians 10:31

April 14, 2019

Eden and my dear mom enjoying Chick-fil-A over the weekend one evening. I love that they play Christian music and Eden always asks me when I take her to wash her hands in the bathroom (and you can hear the music well) she will ask "Mama is that a Christian song?" Then I'll try to discern the tune and sing it to her. So special.

Speaking of eating, I discovered who those most adorable spoons were from. My good friend in high school Charise. Thank you Charise. The message was more timely than you know.

❧ HUMOR ❧

Give attention to the public reading of Scripture, to exhortation and teaching.

1 Timothy 4:13

April 15, 2019

Each Sunday Eden and I sit in the back of the church with Meesie (my mom and Eden's grandma). It's such a good time. Eden really seems to enjoy herself. Sometimes too much. I was looking down at my bible and then looked up and saw her on her "cell phone." She might need to be under church discipline after being caught on the phone during Emilio preaching. We laughed hard.

Give attention to the public reading of Scripture, to exhortation and teaching.

1 Timothy 4:13

❧ VALUE ☙

A righteous man has regard for the life of his animal…

Proverbs 12:10

*A*pril 16, 2019

I'm still battling a temple headache on my left side, which I'm sure is related to my thyroid and me not being able to get my dosage right. I've been taking my medicine as the doctor has prescribed, but the pain has not fully lifted, so I'm committing it to the Lord's care (as I have been but I talked to the Lord in depth about it tonight).

Today was sweet nonetheless. We were driving in the car, and I sat in the back seat with Eden (as I always do) when Emilio or someone else (like my mom) is driving. I have come to really enjoy being chauffeured around town. It's a real delight to be able to sit in the back and enjoy Eden Joy. As I was sitting next to her, she was babbling something, and it was just so cute. It was like I could almost picture her back in my womb and hear her chattering inside. There are many times I have told her I would like to put her back in my tummy. I'm sure my mom told me the same thing.

As I listened closely to her, I could tell it was the word "bicycle" that she was saying over and over. She has grown an obsession with the two bikes that are hanging in our garage. They are not children's bikes. They are for adults, but she keeps asking me to "please take them down." I assure her that I will take them down one day very soon.

I wonder what her fascination with the bikes is all about? But it's precious that something I have minimal regard for, she sees great value in. I almost sold them recently, so it's interesting that she is doing this.

Perhaps today we need to thank the Lord for some of the things around us that have become insignificant. Maybe it's someone or something or even the pet in your home that doesn't get the attention it used to before the children arrived. Give your pet extra love today, and pet them a little longer before you retire to bed. Now I'm convicted. I think I'll go do just that now to my dear pup, Lilly.

A righteous man has regard for the life of his animal...

Proverbs 12:10

❧ JOY ❧

The precepts of the Lord are right, rejoicing the heart.

Psalm 19:8

April 20, 2019 (night before Easter Sunday)

Eden found a 1913 Bible from my family and there was a little note inside that I wrote with a description of who it belonged to. It was my great grandmothers. I asked Eden what was on the note and if she could read it to me. And she said it she would read it and pretended to and said, "It says: gives joy to the heart." Then she kept repeating that over and over. "Gives joy to the heart....Gives joy to the heart." And I said, "You are right, the bible indeed does give "joy to the heart."

Eden's been battling a cough and tonight after our family devotional I was giving her a little bit of oatmeal with some blueberries because she's also been constipated again. I was surprised because she opened up her mouth really big to take the bite (which I was so pleased with, especially since she doesn't seem to like oatmeal much) everything was going great until all of a sudden she made this cough sort of gagging noise and out came the blueberry and the oatmeal. I knew she would be fine and it was as if she needed to cough right when she took the bite but poor Emilio he didn't know what was going on and he nearly screamed. I'm writing this with Eden in front of me in my room, next to my light blue rocking chair, and I'm reading it out loud to her as I write and we are both cracking up over the thought of it all. I think I retold what she did about 7 times. It's good to laugh like this. And we laughed hard. Thank you, Lord, for laughter (Proverbs 17:22).

Before bed Eden looked in the dresser mirror and touched her hair and said "Mama, I think Eden's hair is long." And how true that is! Time has gone so fast. I'm not sure where it has gone. She was just a baby yesterday. I'm still in denial over it all. But I thank God for the time.

The precepts of the Lord are right, rejoicing the heart.

Psalm 19:8

❧ RISEN! ☙

He is not here, for He has risen, just as He said. Come, see the place where He was lying.

Matthew 28:6

---

*A*pril 21, 2019 *(Easter Sunday)*

We couldn't go to church today because Eden has been under the weather so we tried to make the best of it and made these refreshing waters (just looking at them makes us feel better), we dressed up as if we were going to church and sat in the sun a little bit as we listened to worship. Hope you all are having a good Resurrection Day! He is risen and will one day put an end to all our sicknesses. Amen.

❧ FINAL THOUGHTS ☙

The light of the eyes rejoices the heart and good news puts fat on the bone.

Proverbs 15:30

This last portion contains quotes that have ministered to me since Eden's birth. I pray these final thoughts will be imprinted on your heart and mind.

They are taken from *Joyful Mothers*, my friend Rachel Zwayne's Facebook group.

Her page is filled with quotes and wise nuggets that have carried me many days. In between the quotes I might insert a few words or a prayer or just some thoughts on the topic being discussed.

Rachel is Ray Comfort's daughter, a mother of five and wife to Emeal Zwayne (EZ) of LivingWaters.com. I've known her for close to 20 years. Her husband EZ officiated Emilio and my wedding ceremony many years ago. She and her husband also provided us with pre-marital counseling long before Eden came into the world. Rachel's example and wisdom are certainly to be followed.

So, enjoy these wise words. Let them carry you, exhort you, inspire you, wash you, convict you, admonish you and comfort (pun intended) you in your walk with the Lord. Let's dive in!

"Spend a few minutes on Instagram looking at the latest home decorating designs and tips, and you might start looking around your house and feel a bit inadequate and discontent. The key to making your home a place of beauty is to remember what is most important. God has given you all the grace you need to make your family's place of shelter into a haven of love and a refuge from the storms of life. Your first priority is the spiritual atmosphere of your home. If that is your main focus, then your home will overflow with beauty, and if you happen to be able to spruce things up with some cute decor, then that's a nice bonus, but definitely not what will count for eternity." ~ Rachel Zwayne

This quote cut me to the heart as lately, I've really wanted to try to decorate my home better. Like with things that actually match.

Everything (almost everything) has been gifted to us. And so I thought I'd spend a little extra money on re-doing things and boy can it become all-consuming. Once you start one thing you want to change another. Once you look "a little" online you begin to want a whole new house. My mom is in her 70's and came over several times after I painted and redecorated my entryway and she never noticed anything different. All she noticed was Eden and me. That has left a mark on my discontented heart, namely that people are more important than decor and things. Things will perish, and investing time with people will carry on into eternity. Help us, Lord, to not waste time. Not that we can't enjoy making things beautiful, but give us wisdom on how to make our hours count for what matters and for what is lasting and help us to worship You as we do beautify things, but may it not engross us. "So teach us to number our days, that we may present to You a heart of wisdom." Amen.

"Through wisdom a house is built, and by understanding it is established; by knowledge the rooms are filled with all precious and pleasant riches." (Proverbs 24:3-4)

"As parents, we all have different convictions about how we raise our children, and that's a wonderful thing! We are free to seek the Lord for His guidance for our families and walk forward in confidence, knowing that He has given us all the grace we need to lead our children." ~ Rachel Zwayne

"As we navigate this parenting journey, most of us would agree that the teenage years can be filled with insecurity, uncertainty, and confusion for our children. God has given us the responsibility of nurturing and training our children in His ways, which means we must protect them from outside influences that may be detrimental and counterproductive to what we are attempting to sow into their lives spiritually during these vulnerable years. One influence that can be a danger is social media and the Internet." ~ Rachel Zwayne

"As you make internet decisions for your children, my plea is that you are sure—you are sure that each and every freedom you have given your children in this regard is a wise one. You are the adult. You have wisdom gained from experience. Are the places that your child visits online wise and beneficial? Are you swayed emotionally to allow certain freedoms because you want to keep the peace? Ask yourself the hard questions and BE SURE. If you have doubts, don't dismiss them! Err on the side of caution. Spend some time on Instagram (and other media that your children have access to) and be sure that you are completely aware of the images and messages that are being fed to your children day after day (Philippians 4:8)." ~ Rachel Zwayne

Wow. So true. How easily we can fall into this even for ourselves. If we don't have high standards for ourselves then why would we for our children? Let's have a different spirit than the world and make this our aim. "I will set no worthless thing before my eyes; I hate the work of those who fall away; It shall not fasten its grip on me." (Psalm 101:3)

"We have no control over how rapidly the world is changing when it comes to the Internet, but we do have control over the access that our children have to it. We may all come to different conclusions in this regard, but let's all BE SURE that our conclusions are wise." ~ Rachel Zwayne

"Finally, brothers and sisters, whatever is true, whatever is noble, whatever is right, whatever is pure, whatever is lovely, whatever is admirable— if anything is excellent or praiseworthy—think about such things." (Philippians 4:8)

"It has always amazed me how God has created us to have the ability to release emotions by releasing water from our eyes. As a woman, it's hard to imagine what I would do with my emotions if I couldn't express them through tears. So if you need to cry today, do it! It's a gift from the Lord for us to be able to respond to internal pain and stress this way. Let the tears roll, remembering that He is the God of all comfort... then afterward, take a deep breath, and press on in His grace." ~ Rachel Zwayne

"You have taken account of my wanderings; Put my tears in Your bottle. Are they not in Your book?" (Psalm 56:8)

"Teenagers are prone to many ups and downs emotionally. Be sure that you're holding on tight to the Lord, Who is our Rock, and you won't ride the roller coaster with them. You'll be stable, unmoved by their moods, and ready to speak words of wisdom, hope, and love." ~ Rachel Zwayne

"He only is my rock and my salvation; He is my defense; I shall not be moved." (Psalm 62:6)

"Remember the word that the conqueror Caesar always used to his soldiers in a battle. He did not say 'Go forward,' but 'Come.' So it must be with you in training your children. They will seldom learn habits which they see you despise, or walk in paths in which you do not walk yourself. He that preaches to his children what he does not practice, is working a work that never goes forward. It is like the fabled web of Penelope of old, who wove all day, and unwove all night. Even so, the parent who tries to train without setting a good example is building with one hand, and pulling down with the other." ~ J. C. Ryle

"Love should be the silver thread that runs through all your conduct. Kindness, gentleness, longsuffering, forbearance, patience, sympathy, a willingness to enter into childish troubles, a readiness to take part in childish joys. These are the cords by which a child may be led most easily, these are the clues you must follow if you would find the way to his heart." ~ J. C. Ryle

I love that last line from Ryle. A child is easily led when we are gentle and loving and kind (for the most part). When Eden has a lousy attitude, I make sure to talk to her extra sweet, and she melts. However, if I'm irritable and impatient or hurried or anything of the like then she is as well. Or her attitude escalates in the wrong direction. I must always check myself if I find that she is having off days and reason with her. God is a god of reason, and I thank him that we are reasonable beings.

"Come now, and let us reason together," says the LORD, "Though your sins are as scarlet, They will be as white as snow; Though they are red like crimson, They will be like wool." (Isaiah 1:18)

"We should never be afraid that the gentleness of the Spirit means weakness of character. It takes strength, God's strength, to be truly gentle." ~ Jerry Bridges

I can't conquer enough. Being a mom has really tested the fruit of the Spirit in my life. I need His strength every hour of the day. Thankfully, God is rich. Rich is what I need daily, namely grace, grace, and more grace. There are days I feel like I've tapped His grace storage dry, but these verses are a comfort to my weary heart:

"That in the ages to come he might shew the exceeding riches of his grace in his kindness toward us through Christ Jesus." Ephesians 2:7

"In whom we have redemption through his blood, the forgiveness of sins, according to the riches of his grace;" Ephesians 1:7

"Unto me, who am less than the least of all saints, is this grace given, that I should preach among the Gentiles the unsearchable riches of Christ;" Ephesians 3:8

"Your hope as a parent is not found in your power, your wisdom, your character, your experience, or your success, but in this one thing alone: the presence of your Lord. The Creator, Savior, Almighty, Sovereign King is with you. Let your heart rest. You are not in this parenting drama alone. Your potential is greater than the size of your weaknesses, because the One who is without weakness is with you, and he does his best work through those who admit that they are weak but in weakness still heed his call." ~ Paul Tripp

What a great quote and reminder for us daily to walk in.

"For Christian parents, three important aspects of raising children in this day and age are prayer, protection, and preparation.

—We must PRAY fervently for our children for the challenges that they will face in life, and for them to come to know and serve their Creator.

—We must PROTECT our children from a world that glamorizes sin and an evil one who wants to destroy them. Protection should come in the form of vigilance to guard the eyes and ears of our children from the bombardment of evil that comes through television, movies, and the Internet. Our children also need our protection when it comes to their friendships. We must be willing to separate them from friendships that are, and could end up being, harmful.

—We must PREPARE our children to face the challenges of a dark world by pouring God's Word into them, and speaking openly and honestly about even the most difficult of subjects, thus making ourselves a safe place for them to come and communicate their concerns and struggles." ~ Rachel Zwayne

The task of a mom can sometimes be overwhelming, but if we seek God's face and strength each day at a time, He will help us and carry us each day. Try not to get overwhelmed with the future. Let's just take it a day at a time.

"Parents, teach your children that the behavior and attitudes you expect from them are built on something! Don't say, 'Just do it.' As they get older help them see that the standards of thought and attitude and action and entertainment and ministry and mercy are all built on the mercy of God

in Christ. Help them see that Christian living is not a list of do's and don'ts; it is a way of showing the glory of God and Christ. Help them see that Christian living — for children and teenagers and adults — is built on the gospel — on the beauty of Christ crucified and risen and reigning. The question is not mainly, 'What's wrong with this music or this movie or this party or this dress or these drugs or these friends?' The question is, 'How can I act and speak and feel so that I help my friends see the worth of Jesus above all music and movies and parties and friends? How can I live to show that Jesus didn't come into the world to help me party better but to help me love better and die better?'"
~ John Piper

I love this. It's important for us to instruct our children. We are not called to be dictators but rather we are called to be directors. To direct our children in the way of truth and to the One who is "The Way the Truth and the life" (John 14:6).

"We are fast moving on through this world. Soon all that will remain of us will be the memories of our lives. No part of our work will then afford such a true test of our living, as the memorials we leave behind us in our homes. No other work that God gives any of us to do is so important, so sacred, so far-reaching in its influence, so delicate and easily marred—as our home-making. This is the work of all our life—that is most divine. The carpenter works in wood, the mason works in stone, the smith works in iron, the artist works on canvas—but the homemaker works on immortal lives. The wood or the stone or the iron or the canvas may be marred, and it will not matter greatly in fifty years; but let a tender human soul be marred in its early training, and ages hence the effects will still be seen. Whatever else we slight, let it never be our home-making. If we do nothing else well in this world, let us at least build well within our own doors." ~ J.R. Miller

What a sobering thought that we are moving though this world fast. But you don't need me to tell you that. You are well aware of it. It's like oil in our hands. May we have an eternal mindset in our mother-hood. To always have eternity on our eye lids. This can be as simple as waking up and praying with our child or reading a scripture each morning with them, or passing out a tract to the person at the store, or having a song of praise in our hearts as we clean.

"When we are stretched to our limit in mother-hood, we are tempted to despair, but we must not lose heart! The path is bumpy and exhausting at times, but our Guide is good, and kind, and faithful. He is at work in you on this journey. Keep pressing on behind Him, and you will find the rewards along the way to be priceless." ~Rachel Zwayne

"For this is God, our God forever and ever; He will be our guide even to death." (Psalm 48:14)

"It's important to make the mental/spiritual shift from viewing parenting as a series of unrelated corrective encounters to viewing parenting as a life-long connected process. Seldom is change the result of a dramatic moment. So you have partial conversations and unfinished moments, but in each moment you are imparting wisdom to your child, each moment you are exposing your child's heart, each moment you are building your child's self-awareness, each moment you are enlivening your child's conscience, each moment you are giving your child great God-awareness, each moment you are constructing a biblical worldview for your child, and each moment you are giving the Spirit of God an opportunity to do things in and for your child that you cannot do. The wise Father of you and your children designed parenting to be a bit-by-bit, piece-by-piece process. He has called you to take advantage of the little moments of life to take little steps with your children... Here's what parenting is: it's unfinished people (we parents) being used of God as agents of transformation in the lives of unfinished people." ~ Paul Tripp

I can tend to get so caught up just in the moment and forget there is a future ahead. This is a good and timely reminder from Paul Tripp for all us.

"I don't know about you, but I am daily tempted to worry for my children (and future grandchildren!) as I see and hear of all the wickedness in the world around me. When I experience these temptations, I can allow myself to spiral deeper and deeper into anxiety, or I can choose to hold on to the life-changing words of our Savior, and then turn my focus back to my ministry of motherhood."~ Rachel Zwayne

This is me often.

I lose sleep over it at times.

When I was expecting Eden, I was out shoe shopping with Emilio. While he looked for shoes, I passed out gospel tracts to redeem the time. I handed a tract to a man who worked at the store. He was probably in his 70's. I walked away and minutes later felt a tap on my shoulder, and turned around to find the gentleman holding the tract with tears in his eyes.

He said he was saved and "worried for his grandchildren in this generation" and he began to cry harder.

At the time it touched me, but I didn't have the understanding that comes with having children as Eden was still in my womb...but now I get it. Now I understand his tears and his anguish. That dear man's face still has left its mark on my heart.

And you know what comforts me, and I wish I would have quoted to him at the time? Psalm 119:90 that says, God's "faithfulness continues throughout all generations" and that He "established the earth, and it stands."

Wow. What a thought.

He "established the earth" and it "stands" it is nothing (absolutely nothing) for Him to care for our generation and our children's. Rest on that.

"Peace I leave with you, My peace I give to you; not as the world gives do I give to you. Let not your heart be troubled, neither let it be afraid." (John 14:27)

"The command given here in this verse to "forsake not your mother's teaching," insinuates that there is something very significant to forsake. So our prayer should be that when it's all said and done, the teaching that our children remember most from us would be made up mostly of the words of life from the Giver of life." ~ Rachel Zwayne

"My son, observe the commandment of your father And do not forsake the teaching of your mother." (Proverbs 6:20)

Below is a quote I have read many times over. Let's redeem the time, forget the past, press on to know the Lord and know that tomorrow is a new day.

God bless you all for your time and for reading this book (especially if you made it this far). I am so grateful for each of you, dear readers. Here's the quote:

"We all know that our babies are growing fast. There will be that one last time that you carry each of your children, and "last times" for many other precious mommy and child moments. It cuts deep into my heart to think about this, but the pain helps me to cherish the time that God has given me to love and nurture my children. And it is also a reminder that for those of us who are Christ's, one day there will be no end to the things that we wish could last forever." ~ Rachel Zwayne

---

The light of the eyes rejoices the heart and good news puts fat on the bone.

Proverbs 15:30

☞ WORSHIP THE KING ☜

The secret to contentment and joy, and a happy home

Here is a list of various worship songs that Eden and I sang, danced, and listened to daily for the first two years of her life:

Freedom Kids on YouTube:

- Joy of the Lord is Your Strength
- Rejoice Rejoice Rejoice O Daughter of Zion (Eden would dance very hard to this song especially when she was around a year and a half old. We would invite family over and have a dance party)
- ABC Song
- Let's Sing the New Testament

Steven Curtis Chapman:

- Amen (I estimate I have sung this song to Eden 100 times, mostly at nap time)
- Do Everything (A favorite of Eden's)
- Let Us Pray (A favorite of mine from when I was first saved)
- Warrior
- Remember to Remember (I rarely can listen to this without crying)
- Next Five Minutes
- Hark the Herald (Eden says she will sing this at church for her third birthday)

- Christmas Time is Here (Very hopeful song)
- This Baby (I'm relatively certain Eden initially thought this song was about her. Hopefully, my explanations made her understand the song was about the Lord)

Keith and Kristen Getty:

- Go Tell It (Eden loves to "play" her violin with this song. I bought it for her when she was 14 months old)
- May the People's Praise You (This song is the cry of my heart – that all my family will praise the King)
- Come People of the Risen King
- O Church Arise (I sang this song over and over on our evening walks. Eden would sing the "shine" lyric as loud as she could. And whenever we walked by a house with an American flag, we would sing "America, America God shed His grace on thee!" It's become our summer tradition.)
- Lift High the Name of Jesus (Lord, may all of our children want to lift high the name of Jesus)
- Living Water

Phil Wickham:

- Joy
- The Lost Get Found
- Heaven and Earth
- Eden

I Am They:

- From the Day
- King of Love

Matt Redman:
- When We All Get to Heaven
- Undignified

Rizers:
- John 3:16
- Make a Joyful Noise

LifeTree Kids:
- All Around the World
- Jump

For King and Country:
- Glorious

Sovereign Grace Music:
- He is Our God
- I Lay it All
- O Lord, My Rock and My Redeemer
- We Look to You
- Jesus, There's No One like You
- Spirit of God

Sovereign Grace Kids:
- Ready, Set, Go!
- Get Ready

Happy Children:
- Deep, Deep, Deep

Seeds Family Worship:

I cannot say enough good things about this group. All of their songs are Bible verses set to catchy tunes. I thank God for their ministry as their songs carried me through Eden's first two years of life.

- Teach Them
- The Good Song
- Do Not Be Anxious
- Grace
- Eternal Life
- Song for Joy
- Treasure
- The Word of the Lord
- Do Not Fear
- Cast Your Cares
- Refuge and Strength
- SAVIOR

Listener Kids:

- Praise Ye the Lord Hallelujah (New version)
- Jesus Loves Me (Eden sang this one day when we were visiting our local library. So much for being quiet!)

Jason Waller:

- Hark the Herald (This became Eden's favorite song during Christmastime when she was two years old. It was a joy to hear her sing about 50 words of it on her own)
- Joy to the World

Chris August:

- Jesus Savior

Chris Tomlin (written by Andrew Peterson):

- I Lay Me Down (Eden would request this song and say, "Mama, is he a Christian? Because he loves the Lord.")

- Is He Worthy? (This song my friend Kristen sent to me. I cried when I heard it. Eden can sing almost the whole thing, We like Shane and Shane singing it as well)

Go Fish:

- 10 Commandment Boogie (Great way to teach about the 10 Commandments)

To this end also we pray for you always, that our God will count you worthy of your calling, and fulfill every desire for goodness and the work of faith with power, so that the name of our Lord Jesus will be glorified in you, and you in Him, according to the grace of our God and the Lord Jesus Christ

2 Thessalonians 1:11-12